THE ETHICS OF MEMORY

THE ETHICS OF MEMORY

AVISHAI MARGALIT

HARVARD UNIVERSITY PRESS
Cambridge, Massachusetts
London, England

Printed in the United States of America

Third printing, 2004

First Harvard University Press paperback edition, 2004

Library of Congress Cataloging-in-Publication Data

Margalit, Avishai, 1939–
The ethics of memory / Avishai Margalit.
p.   cm.
Includes bibliographical references and index.
ISBN 0-674-00941-x (cloth)
ISBN 0-674-01378-6 (pbk.)
1. Memory (philosophy)—Moral and ethical aspects.   I. Title.

BD181.7 .M37   2002
121'.3—dc21   2002068583

To Shaul and Lia

PREFACE

T HE PROUSTIAN Madeleine cake that triggered my search and research into the memory of the lost past was a little story published in a Jerusalem local newspaper. It was about an officer who did not remember the name of a soldier who was killed under his command. The officer was reproached for failing to remember the name. I tell this story in my first chapter and deal rather extensively with its implication. The point of mentioning it here is to say that nothing big triggered my interest in the ethics of memory. But then again, there *is* something big and terrifying lurking beyond it all.

From early childhood, I witnessed an ongoing discussion between my parents about memory. It started at the end of the war. My parents were in British-ruled Palestine, and their worst fears during the war turned out to be true. Their huge families in Europe were destroyed. I do not remember the actual words they used to talk about it, but I do remember that they referred to it with the traditional term *destruction (hakhurban)*—the way Jews traditionally referred to the destruction of the Temple by the Romans, who then drove them into exile.

As I reconstruct my parents' debate, it went like this:

MOTHER: The Jews were irretrievably destroyed. What is left is just a pitiful remnant of the great Jewish people [which for her meant European Jewry]. The only honorable role for the Jews that remain is to form communities of memory—to serve as "soul candles" like the candles that are ritually kindled in memory of the dead.

FATHER: We, the remaining Jews, are people, not candles. It is a horrible prospect for anyone to live just for the sake of retaining the memory of the dead. That is what the Armenians opted to do. And they made a terrible mistake. We should avoid it at all cost. Better to create a community that thinks predominantly

> about the future and reacts to the present, not a community that is governed from mass graves.

My book is not about my parents' discussion. It is not a book about the Holocaust. But philosophy, some philosophy, starts at home. And my parents' debate hovers above the abyss of my concern with memory and the obligations—if there are any—to remember; or, for that matter, to forget and forgive.

There are two styles of philosophers: *e.g.* philosophers and *i.e.* philosophers—illustrators and explicators. Illustrators trust, first and foremost, striking examples, in contrast with explicators, who trust, first and foremost, definitions and general principles. Explicators may use examples, but their examples are stylized and are more like those that appear after *i.e.* than the genuine examples that follow *e.g.* The illustrators, for their part, run the risk of using examples as little anecdotes that serve no philosophical purpose. The dangers of each style are clear and almost unavoidable; yet, I believe that style in philosophy matters greatly. When examples are apt, they are illuminations, not just didactic illustrations. When definitions are good, they are explications, not mere stipulations. I see merit in both styles, but by temperament if not by conviction I subscribe to *e.g.* philosophy.

My examples, however, are just meant to make a philosophical point or to highlight philosophical distinctions. They are not empirical data in search of empirical hypotheses. In any case they are not primarily designed to serve as such data. For my purpose, an example taken from a work of fiction can make my point just as well as an example taken from a work of history.

This book emerged out of various lecture series: the Horkheimer lectures in Frankfurt, as well as a lecture in Ringberg Castle; the Simon Weil lectures in Melbourne and Sydney and the Bertelsmann lectures at Oxford; Henry Crowe's lecture at Toronto and the Spinoza-Lenz Prize lectures in Amsterdam and Leiden.

To all those in these audiences who voiced their criticism and came up with searching questions I owe a great deal. I have tried to retain in this book the style and form of lectures, keeping learned references to a minimum. This by no means expresses a lack of gratitude to all those whose work I have read and who have influenced my thinking. I am particularly grateful to Menachem Brinker, David Hyed, and Amelie Rorty as well as the generous referees who read the manuscript and gave me very helpful suggestions.

Edna Ullmann-Margalit shared the agony and joy of thinking and writing this book. To both its form and substance she made a valuable contribution, for which I am grateful.

CONTENTS

Memory in Prison

THE IDEA that we are imprisoned in this world is "half as old as time." This idea can be found as early as the Gnostic sectarian teachings of the second century A.D. Gnosticism purports to offer knowledge of the hidden truth about reality as the key to man's salvation. And yet the Gnostic teaching that the world is a prison and the body a prison cell is a metaphor gone wild. Gnostic writers competed with one another in adding more and more walls to their world-prison, as well as more and more wicked jailers to prevent the spirit from escaping in order to unite with the forces of light. But in spite of the top-security jail that the Gnostics concocted in their feverish imaginations, they nevertheless adhered to the possibility of knowing the way out of the maze of this corrupt world, and of reaching the true reality outside.

The formative prison metaphor in philosophy, however, is Plato's parable of the cave. Here too the idea is that there is redemptive knowledge of the outside, a metaphysical knowledge of the ultimate true reality. But if in the search for this knowledge we never know what we are looking for, how can we tell when we have found the thing we are in search of? Plato leads us to conclude that, way back in the past, we knew what we were looking for but then somehow forgot it. The search for knowledge is therefore an exercise in reminiscence, that is, an effort to recall and recollect that which we once knew.

In our own time, the formative metaphor is not Plato's cave but rather Freud's prison. In his prison ward of the unconscious, disturbing memories are locked up by a censor-jailer. They are removed from consciousness, but they are not destroyed; Freud's metaphor is the prison of repression, not the guillotine of forgetfulness.

In Freud's prison, however, there is not one ward but two: one for the unconscious, which is stringently guarded by the censor, and the other for the preconscious, which is guarded in a more relaxed way. In short, Freud's psychic world, like Dante's cosmos, has three compartments: hell, purgatory, and the Eden of consciousness. Later in his life Freud went even further, seeing the unconscious as imprisoning not only troubling memories but harmful fantasies as well. This is an important development. But I shall stick to the earlier metaphor because it is the one that made such a strong impression on our culture.

Freud's prison metaphor commits what Anthony Kenny calls the homunculus fallacy. It explains the individual by positing an entity or a function with the same make-up and complexity as the individual to be explained. The censor-jailer is not a membrane that mechanically blocks undesirable substances from getting into the wrong places in the body. The censor, in Freud's account, is endowed with full interpretative ability to understand the content of the memories and to assess what in them might be threatening to the person it is trying to shelter. In short, this censor is just a little man inside the big man it tries to defend. But this little man is as much in need of an explanation as the big one.

However, the explanatory power of the censor is only one of our concerns. The more serious one, in my view, is Freud's belief in the healing power wrought by bringing repressed memories to the light of consciousness. In Freud's model, repressed memories are subversive agents that cause dysfunctional behavior and even bodily symptoms in the individual. Those who suffer from repressed, traumatic memories might overreact to events in the present. Thus, in the popular press we read accounts that attribute Madeleine Albright's overreaction to Slobodan Milosevic to her traumatic, unacknowledged memories of being a Jewish girl during the Second World War.

Freud himself compares the neurotic person's disproportionate reactions to those of a Londoner who stands in front of the monument commemorating the great London fire of 1666 and, instead of celebrating the vibrant city he encounters today, starts crying for the burnt city of three centuries ago.[1] When secular Jews see Orthodox Jews wailing over the destruction of the Temple two thousand years ago, as if nothing has happened since, they view this behavior as being akin to that of the weeping Londoner in Freud's story.

The idea that disturbing unconscious memories play tricks on us, and that we can recover these memories through the hard work of analysis, is no news. Indeed, it takes pernicious cases, like the so-called repressed memory syndromes of children in California who supposedly recovered memory many years later and accused their parents of sexual abuse in childhood, to draw our attention to how powerful the memory-prison metaphor actually is. Freud himself, to his great yet insufficiently acknowledged credit, warned against just such use—or rather abuse—of the prison metaphor. Still, what permeates our culture today is a rather crude and manipulative version of this picture.

What concerns me, however, is not the healing power of knowing the truth in the case of the individual but the healing power of knowing the truth in the case of communal memories. Crude as it may be, the image of the memory-prison is relatively new with respect to *collective memory*. According to this idea, the French people, for example, with the help of that great censor Charles De Gaulle, in their attempt to protect the glory of France from the shameful memories of Vichy, repressed those memories and removed them from the public space. These repressed Vichy memories then played subversive tricks on the French people, thereby helping to create the neurotic behavior of France after the war. Making the traumatic, repressed communal memories open, explicit, and conscious is said to have healing power. We are asked to believe that this is the only way to overcome the irrationality that springs from past traumas, and the only way to gain peace of mind.

This belief, based on the prison metaphor, is at the heart of the Truth and Reconciliation Committee in South Africa, which was established with the hope that it will lead to social catharsis—that the truth about the past will, by being revealed, bring reconciliation.

Still, memory breathes revenge as often as it breathes reconciliation, and the hope of reaching catharsis through liberated memories might turn out to be an illusion.

There is a very good moral reason to seek truth and, even better, to seek reconciliation. But the idea that truth by itself will bring about reconciliation is a doubtful empirical assumption, based on the memory-prison metaphor.

So far I have talked of metaphors and images rather than arguments and premises. This is as it should be. Our thinking about memory is in the grip of powerful images, or primitive models, like the memory as prison or as storehouse. I share Wittgenstein's belief that the first philosophical move should be to loosen the grip of the metaphor, by being aware that it *is* a metaphor. I shall return to this idea, which guides my discussion throughout this book.

My Topic

The topic of this book is the ethics of memory, with a question mark: Is there an ethics of memory? I consider this topic distinct from the closely related subjects of the psychology of memory, the politics of memory, and even the theology of memory. I believe that it is an important question to ask and not merely a futile administrative exercise in channeling issues to this or to that intellectual department.

My question, Is there an ethics of memory? is both about microethics (the ethics of individuals) and about macroethics (the ethics of collectives). What I want to address can be rendered by a series of questions: Are we obligated to remember people and events from the past? If we are, what is the nature of this obligation? Are remembering and forgetting proper subjects of moral praise or blame? Who are the "we" who may be obligated to remember: the collective "we," or some distributive sense of "we" that puts the obligation to remember on each and every member of the collective?

In the course of these chapters, I reach the conclusion that while there is an ethics of memory, there is very little morality of memory. The drift of this idea—perhaps more appropriately expressed with a question mark than with an exclamation point—obviously hinges on the distinction between ethics and morality. In my account, this in turn is based on a distinction between two types of human relations: thick ones and thin ones. Thick relations are grounded in attributes such as parent, friend, lover, fellow-countryman. Thick relations are anchored in a shared past or moored in shared memory. Thin relations, on the other hand, are backed by the attribute of being human. Thin relations rely also on some aspects of being human, such as being a woman or being sick. Thick relations are in general our relations to the near and dear. Thin relations are in general our relations to the stranger and the remote. (More on this distinction in Chapter 1.)

Ethics, in the way I use the term, tells us how we should regulate our thick relations; morality tells us how we should regulate our thin relations.

I emphasize human *relations* rather than actions and reasons for actions. Of course human relations are manifested in actions, or rather in interactions, that are guided by reasons. But still, the primary concern of both ethics and morality is with certain aspects of human relations. Morality is greatly concerned, for example, with respect and humiliation; these are attitudes that manifest themselves among those who have thin relations. Ethics, on the other hand, is greatly concerned with loyalty and betrayal, manifested among those who have thick relations. These very different aspects merit different accounts, as we will see in more detail in Chapter 1. One account is morality; the other is ethics.

Because it encompasses all humanity, morality is long on geography and short on memory. Ethics is typically short on geography and long on memory. Memory is the cement that holds thick relations together, and communities of memory are the obvious habitat for thick relations and thus for ethics. By playing such a crucial role in cementing thick relations, memory becomes an obvious concern of ethics, which is the enterprise that tells us how we should conduct our thick relations.

Though I confine memory predominantly to ethics, there are cases when morality should be concerned with memory as well. These cases consist of gross crimes against humanity, especially when those crimes are an attack on the very notion of shared humanity. Nazi crimes carried out by an ideology that denied our shared humanity are glaring examples of what morality requires us to remember. Yet, humanity is not a community of memory. Someday it may evolve into one, but today, as a matter of fact—a significant fact—it is not. So who should carry the "moral memory" on behalf of humanity as a whole?

Certainly religions can make a bid on the moral memory of humanity as a whole. Or at least the historical religions can. Judaism, Christianity, and Islam all subscribe to the idea of an autonomous history of humanity that is not merely a part of the cosmic run of events. Man was created for the glory of God, and human history is the goal of creation. It is unfolding under the special guidance of God.

There are secular versions of this picture, to be sure. Hegel's idea of world history with historical laws as a substitute for divine providence is a case in point. But talk about world history does not create a world community of memory. The historical religions claim that they have the potential for creating such a community. The historical

religions aspire to shape humanity as an ethical community. In Chapter 2 I deal quite extensively with one such
aspiration—that of Christianity.

Religion is of relevance here in part because the whole
enterprise of an ethics of memory, as well as the politics of
memory, is under a cloud of accusation that it is merely a
disguised form of religion. The suspicion is that the key
notions of an ethics of memory, such as forgiving and forgetting, get their sense and justification only in the religious context of a forgiving God. And the same suspicion
holds with regard to the politics of memory, which is
viewed as no more than political theology. The most
superficial controversy over erecting a public memorial
monument adds to this suspicion. In Chapter 2 I take this
suspicion seriously and try to disentangle religion from
the ethics of memory as far as it can safely and sensibly be
defended.

Conflating an ethics of memory with religion is my first
worry, though by no means my primary concern. The second worry is of conflating the ethics of memory with traditionalism—that is, conflating the ethics of memory with a
doctrine, policy, or mood that is set to defend tradition.
The connection between traditionalism and the ethics of
memory is straightforward. Traditionalism, by definition,
advocates loyalty to the past. It is the business of the ethics
of memory to work out what this loyalty consists of in

terms of remembering the past. My question is whether doctrines and attitudes that (unlike traditionalism) are oriented toward the future rather than the past can and should be concerned with the ethics of memory. This worry calls for some elucidation.

The counter-Enlightenment thinker Ralph Inge, "the gloomy dean of St. Paul," wrote memorably: "A man may build himself a throne of bayonets, but he cannot sit on it."[2] The way I understand Inge's shrewd dictum is that even the most brutal regime seeks legitimacy, knowing all too well that in the long run terror—which is the sitting on bayonets—is, at the very least, uncomfortable and eventually unbearable.

Mythmakers, epic poets, and chroniclers of the royal court are kept busy trying to provide legitimacy for regimes whose entitlement to govern is anchored in events of the past. Hence the urgent need and the ardent desire of authoritarian, traditional, and theocratic regimes to control collective memory, because by so doing they exercise monopoly on all sources of legitimacy. Thus, there is an intimate relation between traditionalism and nondemocratic regimes.

But do *democratic* regimes also need to recruit memory in order to secure their legitimacy? A democratic regime, so it seems to me, anchors its legitimacy not in the remote past but in current election. It would seem, therefore, that liberal democracies are exempt from an orientation to the past and rest their power on their vision of the future. Dwelling on the past in a democracy is as irrational as crying over spilt milk. Traditionalists would argue, however, that what was spilt in the past was blood, not milk; crying over the spilt blood of your community—much thicker than milk—is what ethical theory is all about.

There is some truth in this crude account of the clash between nondemocratic and democratic regimes, but it is by no means the whole truth. Constitutional democracies, for example, anchor the source of their legitimacy not only in current election but also in a document from the past. A constitution is a constitutive part of the community's shared memory. Moreover, it is not true that the only emotions which fit the democratic spirit are those directed toward the future, like hope. Democracy can and should include backward-looking emotions and attitudes as well, such as forgiveness and gratitude. The reason is that democracy, too, is a systematically ambiguous term. It means, minimally, a technique for changing the government without violence, but it also means a full-fledged way of life. And as a way of life it needs to build among citizens a tradition of loyalty to their shared constitution, institutions, and fair procedures.

In recent history, many cases attest to the tension that arises between these two senses of democracy when a strongly authoritarian regime tries to make the transition to a weak democratic regime. A clash occurs, not just conceptually but in practice, between the impetus to transfer power without violence and the impetus to bring culprits to justice by remembering the past through legal institutions. Transitional justice—how to deal fairly in a newly born or regained democracy that has an undemocratic recent past—is deeply involved with the ethics of memory. Communities must make decisions and establish institutions that foster forgetting as much as remembering. Shredding the personal files of old Stasi (the former East Germany secret services) is an example of a communal decision to forget.

I have mentioned so far two worrisome factors that might lead us to conceive of an ethics of memory too narrowly. One has to do with regarding the ethics of memory as a branch of religion and the other has to do with seeing it as a branch of traditionalism. But I have a third worry. I call it moralism: the disposition to cast judgments of a moral kind on what is unsuitable to be so judged. The wit Elaine May said in her derisively mocking voice, "I love moral problems so much more than real ones." She captured the tedious tendency of moralists to view everything in moral terms.

Calls for an ethics of beliefs or even for an ethics of fiction (which involves appraising novels in moral terms) are, in my view, instances of misplaced morality. Similarly, one should fear the plea to appraise memories in moral terms. Indeed, memory and the ethics of memory can be viewed as a special case of the ethics of belief. The connection is this. To remember now is to know now what you knew in the past, without learning in-between what you know now.[3] And to know is to believe something to be true. Memory, then, is *knowledge from the past*. It is not necessarily knowledge *about* the past. For example, I remember that the Olympic games of 2008 are going to take place in Beijing. I heard about it in the past but the event is going to take place in the future. Indeed, the memory that we need to keep our promises and follow through on our plans is this kind of prospective memory. In any case, to remember is to know and to know is to believe. So, the ethics of memory, if there is such a thing, is part of the ethics of belief, if there is such a thing.

I believe that my distinction between ethics and morality helps to block the expansionist tendency of moralism in the right way. States of mind, attitudes, dispositions, and characters are legitimate concerns in forming our thick relations. Our evaluations of our thick relations are not confined, and rightly so, only to actions, for the simple reason that various psychological states and dispositions that thicken our relations are not just actions. Thin relations are based far more on actions than on attitudes, even though attitudes, such as respect and humiliation, should concern thin relations a great deal too. Our legitimate fear of moralism is met, I believe, by a maneuver of divide and conquer. Divide the subject into ethics and morality and conquer the expansionist tendency of moralism by shifting it to ethics.

The Order of the Chapters

As I indicated in my Preface, the first chapter in this book deals with the implications of remembering personal names as well as remembering persons from our past. As we get older we know very well how troubling this kind of memory, or rather the lack of it, can be. One thing is not in dispute: Remembering names is a clear case of memory. It is also clear that forgetting names can be very annoying. But I shall ask, How can our forgetting of personal names be morally or ethically wrong? I do not want to add insult to injury about not being able to remember names, but I do want to draw some implications from our not remembering the names of persons who, in some important sense, we should have remembered. This will be my starting point.

While there are indisputable cases of individual memories, one may, however, challenge the claim that there are indisputable cases of collective memory. The notion of collective memory, one may argue, is a doubtful extended metaphor. According to this skeptical view, collective memory is an obscure notion in the sense that there are no clear cases to which this notion applies and no clear cases to which it does not apply. In Chapter 2 I probe the ethical and moral implications of the notion of shared memory and its correlative notion, a community of memory.

Whether memory is knowledge or belief, these two "cognitive" notions of memory do not cover the issues that worry those who deal with the ethics and politics, let alone the theology, of memory. Those issues collect, under the heading of memory, something described as *reliving the past*—as distinct from living *in* the past. The notion of reliving the past involves, I believe, various ideas about remembering emotions and especially about remembering emotions with respect to the events and the people remembered. It is not only the sense of the past that we try to recover in our memory but its sensibility. What was it *like* to be in that situation or with those people there and then? In asking this question, Chapter 3 is an effort to distill out of the first two chapters an answer to our basic question, Are there things that, ethically, we ought to remember? The chapter provides a more systematic account of what is involved in ethical assessments and in the idea of a community of memory.

Chapter 4 explores further the issues of remembering emotions and the sense of reliving them. Conveying the sensibility of events from the past that should be landmarks in our collective moral consciousness calls for a special agent of collective memory. Such an agent needs to be invested with special moral authority akin to that of the religious witness or the martyr. The fifth chapter depicts just such a special agent—the moral witness.

An ethics of memory is as much an ethics of forgetting as it is an ethics of memory. The crucial question, Are there things that we ought to remember? has its parallel, Are there things that we ought to forget? Should we, for example, forget for the sake of "forgiving"? This is my topic in the sixth and final chapter.

1

Remember the Name

WHAT'S IN a name? A great deal. Or so I shall argue. My case rests on the most meager memory of a person: remembering her name. Or rather on the horror lest the name be forgotten. Why do we care about that? The memory of a person's name is all we need to get our basic question going: Is there room for an ethics of memory?

The modern man's daily prayer, says Hegel, is reading the daily newspaper. In one of my own daily prayers I came across a report concerning the speedy and problematic career of a certain army colonel. The colonel was interviewed about a publicly known incident in his past, when he was the commander of a small unit. One of the soldiers under his command had been killed by so-called friendly fire. It turned out that the colonel did not remember the soldier's name. There followed a flood of outrage directed at the officer who did not remember. Why wasn't the name of this fallen soldier "scorched in iron letters" on his commander's heart?

I was struck by the moral wrath heaped on this officer simply for not remembering something, and it led me to think about the officer's *obligation* to remember—and if indeed he has an obligation. Let us stay for a while with our little story, as a first crack into the larger issue of obligation to remember in general. Is it really of special importance that the officer did not remember his dead soldier's name? Are there special obligations to remember people's names, or at least some names in certain situations?

On the face of it, asking about remembering the name of the soldier is just a metonym for asking about remembering the young soldier himself. In much the same way, Joseph Brodsky questions the Soviet marshal Zhukov in his poem "On the death of Zhukov": "Did he weep for his men? As he lay dying, did he recall them?"[1]

It seems that the least the officer could, and should, remember is the soldier's name. But had the officer recalled some definite description of the soldier, he would have done just as well—he would have shown that he actually remembered the young man himself. So on the face of it, remembering the name is remembering the soldier, but the obligation, if it is an obligation, is to remember the soldier and not necessarily to remember his name. This claim should be hedged right away. Not just any definite description will do. The required description would present the soldier in a good light or at least in a neutral light. If the description is insulting in some way, it will not work. It will just add insult to injury. "I forgot his name, but I remember him all right. He had a huge red dripping nose" is not a good answer.

Discounting negative descriptions, we are still left with the impression that what the officer was accused of is not remembering the soldier rather than not remembering the name. I think that as far as the case of the officer is concerned, this is true. But then again, I believe there is a powerful picture with respect to remembering personal names that molds our view of memory as an ethical and, I hasten to say, as a religious subject.

David Edgar's play *Pentecost* tells a story of children on their way to a concentration camp.[2] They are squeezed into a cattle truck, so hungry that they eat the cardboard nametags tied to their necks. It is clear that no trace of the children and no trace of their names will be left after they perish. What is so terrifying in this play is not just the knowledge that the children are on their way to be murdered but that they are going to be murdered twice, both in body and in name. This image of the double murder is, I believe, at the core of our attitude toward memory in general, and in particular toward the memory of personal names as referring to the essence of human beings in a way nothing else does.

The Bible is a rich source for this double murder (or double killing) image. The biblical expression "to blot out the name" captures both: "And the lord shall blot out his name from under the heaven" (Deut. 29:20) means both killing the man and destroying the memory of him.[3] There is no doctrine of the immortality of the soul in the Hebrew Bible, but there is, I believe, a distinct idea of the survival of the name as the predominant vehicle for carrying the memory of the dead. The best bearer of a man's name, and the best guarantor of its survival, is the dead man's sons and, by extension, his "seed" (his sons and daughters and their descendants). "Swear now . . . that thou wilt not cut off my seed after me, and that thou will not destroy my name" (1 Sam. 24:21).

Absalom, King David's rebellious son, erects a monument in his own name, saying "I have no son to keep my name in remembrance" (2 Sam. 18:18). It is not clear that there is an etymological connection in Biblical Hebrew between *Zekher* (memory) and *Zakhar* (male), and even less clear that there is any etymological connection between *Isha* (woman, wife) and *Neshia* (forgetfulness, oblivion). Still, there is a strong suggestive association between the words of the first pair, and not merely a phonetic association.

The memorial sanctuary for the Holocaust victims in Jerusalem is famously called Yad Vashem. In September 1942 Mordechai Shenhabi, a member of a secular kibbutz, suggested setting up a memorial under the name Yad Vashem for the Jews murdered in Europe. At the time he made this suggestion, most of the people who were to become victims were still alive. The name Yad Vashem is based on the verse in Isaiah 56:5 which promises a memorial even to the pious eunuch (or castrated man), who is a "dry tree" in the sense that no one will carry his name after his death. "Even unto them will I give in mine house and within my walls *a place and a name* [yad vashem] better than of sons and of daughters: I will give them an everlasting name, that shall not be cut off." God, the ultimate guarantor for the survival of one's name, will establish a memorial place in his city, Jerusalem, so that the names of the eunuchs will survive after them. The eunuch here stands for all those who, without intervention, would leave no trace. By calling the memorial for the Holocaust victims Yad Vashem the idea is expressed that the Jewish victims in Europe are like the eunuchs who leave no trace, and that there will be a national depository for their names, on the model mentioned in Isaiah.

My claim is that in the Bible one's name is not just a

convenient tool for preserving one's memory but is taken as intimately related to one's essence. If the name survives, the essence somehow survives as well. A personal name has the semantic property of designating the same person in each and every possible situation. A personal name is what Saul Kripke calls a *rigid designator*.[4] He coined it as a term of art, but his expression made it to the *Oxford English Dictionary*. A rigid designator refers to the person's essence. That is, it refers to that specific person in all "possible worlds."

A personal name is also perceived in magical thinking not just as expressing but also affecting one's essence. I believe that the peculiar semantics of names is responsible for the magic of names, harming and benefiting by the use of the name. At any rate, the two, semantics and magic, are related.

The idea that the essence of a person is referred to and expressed by a personal name gives the name a particular role in memory. And I believe that the quasi-magical thought of the survival of the name, as the survival of the essence, is what lies behind the doctrine of the double killing: killing the body and killing the name. Thus the biblical metaphors threatening to "destroy" the name (Deut. 7:24), "cut off" the name (Josh. 7:7), let the name "rot" (Prov. 10:7) or "perish" (Psalms 41:15) suggest two killings: one of the body and the other of the name.

What name is remembered may vary with history and

culture. Clifford Geertz tells us of the peculiar use of personal names in the Balinese culture.[5] Each person has a unique, private name made of nonsense syllables, so that there is an unlimited supply of non-repeated names. This name is rarely used and is usually known only to one's elders and peer group, not to younger people. When a person dies, his personal name pretty much dies with him. But there are other means of reference, which for all intents and purposes are just like a personal name—for instance, the use of teknonymous labels ("the father of so and so"). So the Balinese remember one not by a personal name but by means akin to a personal name.

What makes a label akin to a personal name, whether it is a nickname, a definite description, or some other device of that kind, is the fact that the label is without content. Of course some first names have lexical meaning, such as Grace or Gore, and with last names it occurs even more. Think of Green, Good, Gold. The sense in which these names are without content, in my account, means that the meanings of those names in the language do not determine their reference. Mr. Young will be called Young even in old age, and Mrs. Small can be very tall and still referred to by that name. Someone named Gay may not be gay. And so it is with nicknames. "Stumpy" may have been, in her childhood, short and stocky, but now she is tall and lanky, yet Stumpy has stuck with her for life. Its emptiness in terms of content, though not in terms of reference, is what makes personal names and their cognates the last barrier from the abyss of oblivion.

Let us conduct a little thought experiment. If I ask you which you prefer: that a momentous work of yours will survive after your death, but only anonymously, or that your name will survive but none of your works will (as happened to the legendary Dedalus), how would you answer? Miguel de Unamuno, the Spanish philosopher, knew his preference, and believed that he knew yours.[6] He believed that you, as he, would opt for the survival of your name rather than the survival of your work. I don't share his preference, and I don't know your preference. Yet the mere fact that I do not know your preference is enough to underline Unamuno's point: how strong the desire is for even such an insubstantial immortality as that of a name.

It is this strong desire for immortality that religion expresses so forcefully. The source of the wish for an immortal name is not mere vanity. Nor is it merely the desire to "make a name for yourself" in the sense of achieving glory. It is rather a horror of extinction and utter oblivion. The human project of memory, i.e., *commemoration*, is basically a religious project to secure some form of immortality.

Benedict Anderson asks a striking question: Why do we

not erect monuments for the unknown social democrat or for the unknown liberal, as well as for the unknown soldier?[7] The answer surely has to do with the fact that under these labels we do not find "natural" communities of memory, because such ideologies are not engaged in the businesses of immortality, in whatever form. That is both their strength and their weakness. But nations, like religious communities, do. Secular groups, perhaps more than religious groups, face the problem of who will remember the "unheroic dead" (Siegfried Sassoon). It is no accident that Anna Akhmatova blurs the distinction between the secular and the religious by calling her great poem of the Red Terror "Requiem." The anxiety to remember the names is all there. She writes: "I want to name the name of all that host, but they snatched up the list and now it is lost."[8] I would like to distinguish remembering as a religious issue, which I believe to be of utmost importance to the politics of memory, from the ethical issue of remembering.

Memory and Caring

In Edward Albee's *The Play about a Baby*, one of the protagonists tells the audience, in a rather cheerful tone, the following chilling story. He was standing at a party in his house with two young women of very ordinary names. An elderly lady who looked painfully familiar to the speaker approached them. He introduced the young women to the old lady, but when it came time to introduce her to them he was stuck: he couldn't for the life of him remember her name. As the two young women turned away, the old lady chided him: "So my dear boy, you don't remember your mother's name?"

Albee's play is fiction. But if I encountered anyone who, while being in his full mental capacity, with no sudden lapses, and very familiar with his mother, suddenly forgot his mother's name, I would doubt his sanity, not his morality. I would, in Wittgenstein's phrase, feel myself very distant from him. But unlike Albee's case, there is nothing eerie or mad about an officer who does not remember his soldier's name, even if he was the only soldier killed in action. What is at stake here is the officer's *caring*, not his craziness. The point of the story about the officer's forgetfulness is that we take it as a strong indication of not caring about the young soldier.

Our little story about the officer's forgetfulness highlights a triangle of relations that is at the center of an ethics of memory. One side of the triangle connects memory and caring, the second connects caring and ethics, and only then we are ready to connect memory with ethics. This is the path I shall now pursue.

What is the relation between memory and caring? It is,

I maintain, an internal relation—a relation that could not fail to obtain between these two concepts since memory is partly constitutive of the notion of care. If I care for someone or for something, and then I forget that person or that thing, this means that I have stopped caring for him or it. To say that the officer still cares for the young soldier but does not remember him is incoherent. The case of the officer hinges on the index of time. The fact that the officer does not remember him *now* (at the time, say, of the interview reported in the newspaper) does not necessarily mean that he did not care about him *then* (at the time the soldier was killed). But is not the fact that the officer does not remember now at least a strong indication that he did not care then?

In answering this question, let me shift from the army colonel to the enigmatic character of Don Juan. Tirso de Molina, who created Don Juan's literary image in the seventeenth century, viewed him as a religious heretic who did not care at all about the women he seduced and abandoned but used them to express his defiance of the Church. The Don Juan of Ernest Theodor Wilhelm Amadeus Hoffman, on the other hand, is a romantic who cares deeply for the ideal woman but not for the flesh and blood women whom he encounters. In Peter Brook's interpretation of Mozart/Da Ponte's Don Giovanni, he is a man who cares a great deal for each and every woman on his "mille e tre" list of seduction (and that, mind you, is only the number for Spain). However, he cares for them *at the time* of the seduction only; later, he forgets them completely.

Now, is this Don Giovanni psychologically convincing? Infatuation, unlike love, does not require a biographical continuity and therefore does not need to involve memory, whereas love, as a form of caring, does involve memory. Thus, by not remembering, Don Giovanni strongly indicates that infatuation, not love, was the basis for his relationships with women. Brook's interpretation, exciting as it is, is not psychologically convincing to me. One's remembering a person *now* is a strong indication that one cared at the time, at the very least, if not still. And conversely, the officer's not remembering the name of the soldier now is a strong indication that he did not care much for him at the time.

If the relation between memory and caring is internal, it is a complicated notion of internal relation that is involved here. A typical internal relation is constitutive (essential, defining) for both terms in the relation. The relation of "being lighter than," which holds between white and black, is constitutive to both white and black: if the relation does not hold, white would not be white and black would not be black. In the case of memory and caring, on the other hand, caring is not constitutive to memory.

Sometimes we remember people and events we do not

care about. We remember particularly well people we hate, that is, people we do not care about in any positive sense of caring. Or we may care deeply about people of whom we have no memory. One may be separated from one's mother as a baby and not remember anything at all about her and yet care a great deal about her—trying to find her, seeking desperately to be near her, and so on.

So in my account, memory is not a necessary condition for caring, and caring is not a necessary condition for memory. What I do claim is that a conditional sense of memory is necessary for caring: If I both care for and remember Mira, then my remembering Mira is inherent in my caring for her. I cannot stop remembering Mira and yet continue to care for her.

Compare it with the following case: I am today older than my mother was when she died. Her age and my age are contingent facts. But if both she and I live, then my being younger than my mother is inherent in being her son.

Harry Frankfurt sees a conceptual relation between caring and importance.[9] I hesitate. There is no contradiction, in my view, in saying that I care about Arabella but Arabella is not important, or not really important, in the sense of being truly significant in my life and valuable in and of herself. There is not even a contradiction in saying that I care about Arabella but Arabella is not really important *to me*.

The issue, however, remains. Is something important to me because I care for it, or do I care for it because it is important to me? Like Frankfurt, I go with the former: caring confers importance rather than the other way around. I do not care about everything that I deem important; and not everything I care about is important to me. Only those that I care for *on reflection* are important to me. On reflection, I may discard as unimportant, for example, things that dominate my thoughts and feelings that I regard as obsessions of mine. I regard my caring for those things as an obsessive caring. In my reflective moment I might even deny that I "truly" care for them. We may draw a distinction here between caring and concern, and make concern the term for reflective caring. In this view, caring is merely a strong symptom that what we care about is important to us; only concern is conceptually, not just symptomatically, tied to what is important to us. Yet I shall stick to the use of the term *caring* and make it understood as concern.

Like John Austin, I believe in the law of conservation of obsolete meanings for the sake of philosophy. *To care* used to have a meaning now declared obsolete, namely, to mourn. The connotation that connects caring to memory through the idea of mourning is one I would like to preserve. Moreover, *caring*, more than *concern*, suggests regard for other people. True, both words can be used with respect to a variety of things and activities that do not directly involve people. For example, one may care greatly and be deeply concerned about playing Bach on authentic instruments. Yet it strikes me that the word *caring* fits one's feelings for humans better than does the word *concern*. And the sense of *caring* that we need for a discussion of ethics is a caring for people. Subsequently, *caring* and *care* are the words I will use.

Ethics and Caring

Memory, then, blends into morality through its internal relation with caring. And caring, and especially the lack of caring, seems to belong quite naturally to morality. Indeed, some will hasten to add that caring should be regarded as the core attitude of morality.

Against the claim that caring belongs to morality and even constitutes its core, I would like to present a counter claim, according to which we need morality precisely because we do *not* care. That is, we usually lack an attentive concern for the well-being of most members of the human race. We usually care about our parents, children, spouses, lovers, friends, and by extension about some significant groups to which we belong. But by no means do we care about everyone. For most of humanity, most people most of the time are pretty much indifferent. An Oxford worthy was once asked, How do you carry on? "By not caring" was his answer. Most people most of the time carry on by not caring for most other people.

Caring is a demanding attitude toward others. Some of us are by inclination good-hearted people, who may have a diffused benign attitude toward our fellow human beings in general. But this diffused good will does not amount to that unselfish heed to the particular needs and interests of others that caring requires. The snag is not that it is hard to like people we don't know: caring does not necessarily require liking. What we find hard is the *attention* that is implied by caring. Women may be better at dividing their attention than men, and thus more able to care for others than men, as Carol Gilligan used to argue.[10] But even Mother Teresa lacked the resources to pay attention to everyone. Along with Dostoyevsky, we are suspicious of those who care for humanity in general but who do not care for any human being in particular. We should be even more suspicious of those who pay attention only to what *they feel* toward others but are incapable of paying attention to others; in short, we should be suspicious of sentimentalists.

We pay attention not only to our friends but also to our foes. Still, only our friends command our concern for their well-being. We need morality to overcome our natural indifference to others. Indeed, we need morality not so much to counter evil as to counter indifference. Evil, like

caring, is a scarce commodity. There is not so much banality of evil as banality of indifference. Yet, one has to admit that the combination of evil and indifference is lethal,
like the combination of poison and water. In one sense
the claim about the banality of evil refers to this combination.

There is an obvious difficulty with my idea of viewing
morality as an antidote to indifference. Morality on its
own is not motivation enough to overcome the mindless
inertia of our indifference toward the faceless other. Our
general sense of justice and respect for humans as humans does not seem good enough to get us going; as
Hume believed, we need the right doses of sympathy toward our fellow human beings to motivate us. I believe
that this is true, but sympathy is a much weaker attitude
than caring. It does not require the attention and intensity
of caring but a mere free-floating sense of good will.

What does caring care about? It cares about the well-
being of meaningful others. It is concerned with their
wants and needs. It is usually concerned with their rational wants and needs, but in the case of love (as a special
form of caring) we are also tuned to the whims of the beloved. At its best, caring enhances a sense of belonging. It
gives the other the feeling of being secure in having our
attention and concern, irrespective of their achievements.
Caring, in addition to being a sentiment, is an attitude, in

the sense that optimism is an attitude. It is a way of viewing or perceiving as much as a way of doing. It is a selfless attitude.

Heidegger made famous the idea of caring (Sorge).[11] It is for him a basic feature of the human condition. It is a way of living in time. It manifests itself in planning, in looking after someone, in a way that only creatures who have a sense of an open future can care. But whereas Heidegger stresses the essential role of the future in his idea of caring, I stress the importance of the past. When we care about another, we find it natural to expect the other to be one with whom we share a common past and common memories.

Though caring is a selfless attitude as far as our personal ego is concerned, it is not immune to collective egoism, in the form, for example, of tribalism or ethnocentrism. This can turn caring from a noble attitude into a nasty one. We are all familiar with people who care greatly about "their" people and who are ready to make real sacrifices for them but who have utter disregard for those outside the tribe. Unselfish idealism is sometimes responsible for unspeakable cruelty to outsiders.

Caring may also be problematic for the pluralist liberal, because of the inherent tension between caring and individual autonomy. The test of the liberal, in my view, is in his acceptance of another's right to make his or her own big mistakes. It is easy to adopt a tolerant attitude toward mistakes made by people to whom we are basically indifferent. But it is difficult with regard to people we care about, perhaps most of all with regard to our children. It is painful, sometimes unbearable, to watch them waste a distinct talent they have, behave irresponsibly regarding their health, or choose an obviously wrong spouse. Caring may easily play out at the expense of respect for the other person's autonomy. It may turn into emotional blackmail, or even active intervention, so as to prevent the person we care about so deeply from making what to us is so obviously a big mistake. I mention the *price* of caring so as to avoid the sermonizing tone we sometimes assume when talking about its virtues: cheap talk is talk without a price tag attached.

Another important feature of caring is protectiveness. Caring is an attitude that suggests constant worry and apprehension about dangers and failures (think again about caring for one's children). Caring also carries duties and evaluations. I believe, for example, that betraying a friend or lover is a sin against caring. We cannot assume that all people who are close to each other also care about each other. We all know the type who is terribly nice to strangers but horrible to his wife and children. Our moral obligation should be extended to all: to the near and dear as well as to the far and away. But caring is the attitude at the heart of our thick relations. Such relations call for more than mere moral rights and wrongs.

Like others before me (notably Bernard Williams), I make use of the fact that the English language has two terms, *ethics* and *morality*—the first from the Greek, the second from the Latin.[12] Morality, in my usage, ought to guide our behavior toward those to whom we are related just by virtue of their being fellow human beings, and by virtue of no other attribute. These are our thin relations. Ethics, in contrast, guides our thick relations. True, we seldom refer to others as bare human beings. We may refer rather to others as people in distress or in need: the poor, the sick, the old, the orphans and widows. These labels of human distress denote morally relevant aspects of people and call for a moral response. But these labels are not defined from an egocentric point of view. On the contrary, the poor of *my* town, who, according to Jewish law should take precedence in my behavior over the poor in general, are defined by their relation to me.

We may even extend the notion of thick relations to include one's very thick relation to one's own self, which involves a concern with leading a good life. This special case is the meeting point between Williams's notion of ethics as the concern to lead the good life and mine. But the important point for memory is that, because it is enmeshed with caring, memory belongs primarily to ethics, not to morality.

Note that I talk of thick and thin relations and not of thick and thin descriptions, where thick and thin have to do with the interpretations of those descriptions. Thick descriptions are culturally bound and historically sensitive, whereas thin descriptions are more context-independent. "He is saluting" involves thick description. On the other hand, "She is sleeping" involves only a thin one. What counts as recognizing superior rank and giving it a sign (saluting) is content-dependent; what counts as recognizing sleep is not. There is correlation between thick relations and thick descriptions and between thin relations and thin descriptions—correlation, but not identity. One of the things that this might mean is that thin descriptions in reference to thin relations are more amenable to being couched in general principles than thick descriptions of thick relations. If this is true, then we may expect morality to be couched in principles while ethics depends on comparisons to paradigmatic cases. We shall encounter one famous such case shortly—the case of the Good Samaritan.

Ethics might turn out, in Gilbert Ryle's metaphor, to be less like a litmus test and more like a wine tasting, with its constant comparisons to good examples. Ethics seems to be more suitable for what I have called *e.g.* philosophy, and morality for *i.e.* philosophy.

Applying my distinction between ethics and morality to our leading example, the colonel and the fallen soldier, we might say that the officer, if he did anything wrong at all, violated an ethical precept but not a moral one. In blaming the officer, we espouse the idea that in a small combat unit, based on very thick relations of loyalty and shared traumatic experiences, a commander should care for his soldiers not only instrumentally but fraternally as well. It is doubtful, however, whether a fighting officer, of all people, should indeed care about his soldiers in a noninstrumental sense. Of course, we expect a good combative commander to look after the needs of his fighters as fighters, to keep them in good shape and in good spirits. Knowing their first names can be conducive to that goal. But all of this is instrumental care, the aim of which is to ensure the best results on the battlefield.

If by now you have acquired a distaste for officers and army life, think about the more sublimated profession of a medical surgeon. Do you want her to remember the names of all the patients who died on her operating table, despite her best efforts to save them? I bring up these observations in order to convey that I am not interested in the *validity* of the accusation directed at the officer or at the surgeon, but in its *nature*. And its nature, I maintain, is ethical, not moral.

Who Is My Neighbor?

If the scope of morality is the whole human common-wealth, each and every human being, what is the scope of ethics?

It seems that in religious ethics there is tension between the widest possible scope (the scope of morality) and a narrower scope. We can find this tension in the various interpretations of the celebrated injunction "Thou shalt love thy neighbor as thyself" (Lev. 19:18). Jonathan loved David as "his own soul." David compared Jonathan's love for him to the love of women. This is not the kind of attitude we are required to take toward our neighbors, who-ever they are. The "love" in this verse is, I believe, some-thing akin to my sense of caring. But then, who is this neighbor whom we are supposed to love or care for?

Interpretations vary widely and wildly. Take as one ex-treme the sectarian Essenes associated with the Dead Sea Scrolls. Their gloss on "thy neighbor" is a fellow member of one's sect. In their sectarian reading of the scripture, all outsiders are by definition wicked, and an Essene has an obligation to hate them. So "love thy neighbor" is transformed into a cultivated cult of hate toward the world.

On the other pole we find the old rabbi Ben Azzai who sees the commandment to love (care) as extended to all one's fellow human beings.[13] It is not surprising that those who espoused the Jewish universalistic approach, such as Moses Mendelssohn and Herman Cohen, adopted this interpretation of "your neighbor."[14] But this universalistic reading of the verse is far from being the standard interpretation among Jewish commentators.

A far more typical reading of "thy neighbor," shared by no less an authority than Maimonides, regards "thy neighbor" as confined to fellow Jews only. It is against the background of such a nonuniversalistic interpretation that the absorbing story of the Good Samaritan (Luke 10:25–37) takes place.

The Good Samaritan story comes as a direct answer to our question, Who is our neighbor? A man—a Jew—went from Jerusalem to Jericho, and on the way he was attacked, robbed, wounded, and left half dead on the roadside. By chance a certain priest came down that way, and then a Levite. Both were fellow Jews with religious standing, and both "passed by on the other side." Then there came a Samaritan, who belonged to a nation hostile to the Jews, and—as the verse tells us—"took care of him."

Jesus then asked, rhetorically, Who of the three was truly the wounded man's neighbor?

The idea here is that the notion of a neighbor is powerful enough to cross tribal, religious, and ethnic boundaries. The Good Samaritan encountered his fellowman in a face-to-face situation. Witnessing his suffering, "he had compassion on him." It is this physical proximity that brings the New Testament to translate the word *Re'a* in the biblical Hebrew dictum as neighbor, rather than friend, companion, or associate, which are the standard senses of the Hebrew word.

Kant takes up the notion of proximity when he defines neighbors as any fellow human beings "united by nature in one dwelling place so that they can help one another".[15] But then the question arises, What does "one dwelling place" actually mean? If by "one dwelling place" is meant a *stable* dwelling place, and not a place where a mere chance encounter occurs (such as a roadside on the way to Jericho), then the relationship between the people involved would normally be more like thick ethical relations than thin moral relations. This is not what Kant had in mind.

For Kant, being on the same planet with other human beings is enough to make them neighbors. And so a meeting on the way to Jericho of a wounded Jew and a Good

Samaritan makes them neighbors even more. It gives the Samaritan an opportunity to help a fellow human being.

As Hume noticed, there are some circumstances that enhance the chances that a person will gain our sympathy.[16] People who suffer close to us elicit more care and compassion than those who are remote. People who are "like us" are more likely to muster our sympathy than those who are unlike us. Our countrymen engage our sympathy more than foreigners do. Sympathy is a response to suffering, not to success. I can offer sympathy to the one that lost the competition but not to the one who won it. Usually, all these circumstances come together, especially in the historical setting of the New Testament story. That is, living in proximity, being kith and kin, being similar and familiar are correlated features that enhance the chances of mutual sympathy if not full-fledged care. The beauty of the Good Samaritan story is to show that those features may hold but the one who is the true neighbor and who responds to suffering is not the one who bears those features.[17]

In my reading of the story, the Levite, as a fellow Jew, was a neighbor of the wounded Jew who neglected his ethical duty. The Samaritan, on the other hand, was not a neighbor and so had no ethical duty. Yet he responded to a moral duty—and arguably went beyond his moral duty—to help and give comfort to a fellow human being despite being a stranger. So in my interpretation, the priest and the Levite should be assessed in ethical terms and found wanting for their betrayal of a neighbor. In contrast, the Good Samaritan should be assessed in moral terms and found excellent for helping a fellow human being.

In Kant's reading, then, "Love thy neighbor as thyself" is a duty that all human beings have toward one another, whether or not they find the others worthy of their love. Thus, in my terminology, Kant interprets this biblical maxim as a moral maxim. But in my account, love—that is, caring—is a thick relation that can be directed to others only insofar as they are worthy of our love. By "worthy of our love" I do not mean that they possess lovely traits, but that they are people with whom we have historical relations, and not just a brief accidental encounter.

Systematic Ambiguities

The question, Who is my neighbor? hinges on the meanings of the term *neighbor*, which, like the terms *caring*, *person*, and *individual*, are, in the language of Gilbert Ryle, systematically ambiguous. This ambiguity arises because these terms occupy the twin domains of ethics and morality—that is, thick relations and thin ones. Thus, in the context of morality, *neighbor* means a mere fellow human being. But in the context of ethics, a neighbor is someone with whom we have a history of a meaningful, positive, personal relationship, or a history that can be mediated through some imagined community, such as the community of my fellow Jews, most of whom I never encountered in my life.

The scope of ethics is determined by our thick relations, which determine who our metaphorical neighbor is. But then the hard question arises, What thick relations? The actual ones we happen to have, or the one we are assumed to have or ought to have, which might, in their most extensive scope, encompass all of humankind? Thus morality turns into ethics.

I shall come to this vexing question in the next chapter, where I compare the "Christian" project of turning morality into ethics (by making all relations thick) with the "Jewish" project of keeping morality and ethics apart. There is a third possibility—of basing all our relations with others, both near and dear as well as far and foreign, solely on the thin relations of morality. But no one, apart perhaps from the old Stoics, has advocated this position.

Yet many philosophers, inspired by Kant, would deny the distinction between morality and ethics, believing that morality, properly understood, can handle all thick relations as well as the thin ones. This position merits, of course, a serious discussion, which I shall not go into here. But one quick remark can be made, namely that the issue between this Kantian position and mine can easily deteriorate into a pointless quibbling about the word *morality*. It could happen if the Kantian position treats thick relations very differently from thin relations but still insists that both are moral relations.

Caring, too, in the context of morality, can be a thin, ad hoc notion, which may nevertheless be very demanding on the occasion that it is exercised, as the story of the Good Samaritan attests. Still, having paid the inn-keeper to look after the wounded man, the Good Samaritan is free to leave the inn, thereby terminating his accidental relationship with the injured Jew. And so it is with the term *person*. In the context of morality, it means a bare human being, the subject of morality. But in ethical theory, a *person* (or an *individual*) is an achievement word, not an assumption word as it is in moral theory. In an ethical context, a person is someone with personality, and the personality is constituted by memory. Memory, in my account, is not the criterion for personal identity, where the notion of *person* is taken as a thin relation. Rather, memory is crucial for *personality* identity. Personality identity in its anthropological sense is what is required for an ethical theory, and personal identity, in its metaphysical sense, is what is required for moral theory.

Do the notions of memory and remembrance, as I use them, suffer from the same systematic ambiguity as that between morality and ethics? Is there some minimal obligation to remember in the context of morality, too, and not just in the context of ethics? After all, the wounded man would seem to be under a moral obligation of gratitude to the Good Samaritan, the stranger who saved his life. And how can he honor the Samaritan who saved his life if not, at a minimum, by remembering the benevolence and care that was extended to him?

Moreover, isn't the victim morally entitled to impose — if he only could — his memory of what happened to him on his tormentors, that is, on the robbers, as well as on the priest and the Levite who passed by without even a gesture of concern? By extension, are not the Korean "comfort women" morally entitled to impose on the Japanese people their memory of horrific violations at the hands of Japanese soldiers during World War II? Are not the Jews morally entitled to impose the memory of their destruction not only on their German tormentors but also on those that knew and yet did nothing to help? These questions, in the context of communal memory, will be addressed in Chapter 2.

2

PAST CONTINUOUS

Shared Memory

ARE THERE episodes that we ought to remember? Are there episodes that we ought to forget? Let us understand the *we* as the collective or communal we. The two questions thus amount to the question of the ethics of collective memory.

The concept of memory, like the concepts of will and belief, applies primarily to individuals. By this I mean that an interpretive priority is given to the individual sense of the concept over its use with regard to collectives. We can explain to a child the meaning of "The nation remembers its day of liberation" by an appeal to his understanding of what it is for his friend to remember. But we cannot, in normal circumstances, explain to him what it is for his friend to remember by counting on his prior understanding of what it is for the nation to remember. The order of the explanation of meaning reflects the interpretative priority. This in itself does not mean that we may not use collective models in order to understand individuals better. This is, indeed, what Plato does. He uses the state to explain the structure of the individual psyche, believing that the city-state writes in "big letters" what the individual writes in small ones.

Once the mental vocabulary gets going, we are constantly surrounded by hermeneutic loops: we understand collective psychology by appeal to individual psychology, and also the other way round. Take the sentence "The nation remembers its fallen soldiers." The question is not whether it is a metaphor: it is, or at least it is an extended sense of "remembers." The question is whether it is a nondeceptive metaphor. A deceptive metaphor is a metaphor in which dissimilar features from the primary domain, the domain of individual psychology, are carried over and into the secondary domain of collective psychology, along with genuine similar features. Such dissimilar features passing as similar gives a false account about collective psychology. Needless to say, a nondeceptive metaphor is a metaphor that does not deceive us in this way.

For example, collective will is a deceptive metaphor. It carries over, to the domain of the collective, an important dissimilar feature from the individual will, namely, the feature of having a center. Society has no equivalent to the self as center, and therefore the collective will has no focus.[1] This deceptive metaphor, I would add, might turn into a politically dangerous metaphor, if the collective is supplied with a Führer or other leading individual who is postulated as the embodiment of the center of the collective will and the sole guarantor of the unity of the will.

To be sure, not every false picture (or deceptive metaphor) is dangerous. For example, the tendency of some people to slow down their walking pace when they try to remember something and accelerate when they try to forget is harmless enough. The idea seems to be that by slowing down they stay closer to the event they are trying to remember and by accelerating they run away from it. This is pretty much like the magical thinking of gamblers who try to roll a small number on dice by shaking their hand slowly and throwing it tenderly, whereas rolling a high number involves shaking it briskly and throwing it abruptly. But all that, unlike the Führer principle, is more funny than frightening.

At this point let me introduce a distinction between *shared* memory and *common* memory. It is, I believe, a distinction with merit. The people booing Nicolae Ceausescu in the square in Bucharest in December 1989 took part in an event that started an uprising that eventually led to Ceausescu's downfall. Suppose that, contrary to fact, with the help of his brutal secret police (the notorious Securitate), Ceausescu had recuperated and regained power. Given the nature of the terror reigning in Romania at the time, who would have dared mention out loud— or, for that matter, even in a whisper—the event in the square? Everyone in Romania who took part in that episode, or who watched it on television, would remember such a memorable scene. In such a case the memory of the booing in the square would have become a *common* memory but by no means a *shared* one.

A common memory, then, is an aggregate notion. It aggregates the memories of all those people who remember a certain episode which each of them experienced individually. If the rate of those who remember the episode in a given society is above a certain threshold (say, most of them, an overwhelming majority of them, more than 70 percent, or whatever), then we call the memory of the episode a common memory—all of course relative to the society at hand.

A *shared* memory, on the other hand, is not a simple aggregate of individual memories. It requires communication. A shared memory integrates and calibrates the different perspectives of those who remember the episode— for example, the memory of the people who were in the square, each experiencing only a fragment of what happened from their unique angle on events—into one version. Other people in the community who were not there at the time may then be plugged into the experience of those who were in the square, through channels of description rather that by direct experience. Shared memory is built on a division of mnemonic labor.

We are usually unaware of the channels by which we share memories with others, just as we are often unaware of the ways we came to learn certain historical facts. But there are dramatic cases when we actually are aware of such channels. Psychologists are rightly puzzled by these "flashbulb" memories.[2] Most New Yorkers, for example, remember very vividly where they were when they heard about the attack on the World Trade Center and how they heard about it. There is, of course, nothing puzzling in the fact that they all remember the event of the attack itself, which was surely a momentous one in their lives. What is puzzling is that so many people remember trivial items of information that accompanied the attack, such as who told them about it, what precisely they were doing when they were told, and so on. The question is why such details, which usually drop out of memory, are so vividly recalled.

A common explanation is that we remember these details better because, when the event is dramatic, we tend to rehearse the story more often. But I would like to add an explanation, or rather a speculation, of my own, one that ties the phenomenon of the flashbulb memory with shared memory. With regard to dramatic events, we are aware of the channels through which we were plugged into the shared memory. The significance of the event for us depends on our being personally connected with what happened, and hence we share not only the memory of what happened but also our participation in it, as it were. It is not surprising that blacks in the United States have much better flashbulb memories than whites of the assassination of Martin Luther King, Jr., while whites have better flashbulb memories of John Kennedy's assassination.[3] Even if it turns out that flashbulb memories are not on the whole reliable, that fact would not undermine the point that we find it important to report (even falsely) the channels by which we become related to a shared event when that event is of immense importance to us.

In the case of whites' and blacks' flashbulb memories of the assassinations of Kennedy and King, it seems that these two events had a different significance for the two communities. Hence the difference in intensity and perhaps in accuracy between the flashbulb memories of these two groups of people. The flashbulb phenomenon is not necessarily confined to one community of memory. Many people all over the world retained for quite a while a flashbulb memory of Kennedy's assassination. But then many people around the world feel that the role of the

THE ETHICS OF MEMORY

president of the United States is too important to relegate solely to the memories of Americans; certainly many people in Berlin had a strong feeling that they were heavily invested emotionally in Kennedy. Still, when all is said and done, I believe that the Germans are bound to have a much stronger flashbulb memory of the fall of the Berlin wall than we outsiders do.

I mentioned already that shared memory, unlike common memory, is subject to a division of labor, so to speak. In modern societies, characterized by an elaborate division of real labor, the division of mnemonic labor is elaborate too. In traditional society there is a direct line from the people to their priest or storyteller or shaman. But shared memory in a modern society travels from person to person through institutions, such as archives, and through communal mnemonic devices, such as monuments and the names of streets. Some of these mnemonic devices are notoriously bad reminders. Monuments, even those located in salient places, become "invisible" or illegible with the passage of time. Whether good or bad as mnemonic devices, these complicated communal institutions are responsible, to a large extent, for our shared memories.

In the division of labor of shared memory, ordinary lay people may have only a hazy idea about things past. A young man I met in Prague knew vaguely that something awful and sinister happened in Lidice during the war, but he didn't quite remember which war and what exactly happened. What happened was a retaliatory massacre of the male residents of Lidice after the assassination of Reinhard Heydrich, the Nazi governor in Prague, by the Czech underground. This young man, however, is plugged into networks of shared memories that can fill in the missing information. It is less likely, though, that he is plugged into a network that can fill in the details of the retaliatory massacres by the Nazis at roughly the same period in Oradour-sur-Glane, France, or Puten, Holland.

Voluntarism of Shared Memory

In one important sense individual memory is involuntary. The distinction I am invoking is similar to the one we make between voluntary and involuntary muscles. A voluntary muscle can be directly exercised on demand. (We are speaking here of creatures who can respond to a demand and who are properly motivated to do so.) In some sense I can exercise my heart muscles on demand, by starting to run. But this is an indirect method of exercising a muscle. People differ, to some extent, in their ability to move various muscles: at parties people may make us laugh by moving muscles that most of us can't exercise at will, such as those that wiggle ears. But by and large, for normal people, heart muscles are involuntary and hand muscles are voluntary.

Is memory, personal memory, involuntary like the muscles of the heart, or voluntary like the muscles of the hand? It is pretty clear that just being told to "forget it" does not quite secure forgetfulness: if anything, it increases the chance of remembering. And similarly, being told to remember, and being properly induced to recall, is no guarantee that we can do so. We cannot remember on demand. We may of course use helpful, indirect methods of remembering—trying to recall where we last used the keys, where we went afterward, and so on—with the hope that reconstructing what we did will lead us to where we put the lost keys. But such mnemonic heuristic devices are indirect methods of remembering, not instances of remembering on demand.

The relevance of all this to ethics or morality seems straightforward: We cannot be morally or ethically praised for remembering, or blamed for failing to remember, if memory is not under our control. The philosophical cliché has it that *ought* implies *can*, and there is no point in obligating us to do what we cannot do at will. Remembering and forgetting may, after all, not be proper subjects for moral or ethical decrees and evaluations.

On the strength of just this argument, when adapted to belief, John Locke advocated religious tolerance, arguing that since heretics cannot help believing what they believe, they can only be blamed for *acting* on these beliefs, not for having them. Indeed, the argument about the involuntariness of belief, memory, and love played a major role in the attempt to remove states of mind from the realm of moral judgments and to confine morality and ethics to action. If memory and forgetting are not under our control, our original question as to whether there is an ethics or a morality of memory should be a resounding *no*.

However, I believe that the requirement of being able to do something on demand as a test for having it under control is an unreasonably high standard. Consider the case of keeping promises. It is a paradigm case for applying a moral judgment. Yet in order to keep our promises, we have to remember them. Forgetting a promise is at most an excuse, not a justification, for not keeping it. It is commonly required that we see to it that we remember our promises, as much as it is required that we keep them.

But even if we concede the force of the claim that you have no control over your remembering and forgetting and that you are not therefore morally accountable for remembering or forgetting, matters are different when the issue is *shared* memory. Let me explain, taking a somewhat roundabout route. In most cases we cannot commit a Kantian generalization—do something only if everyone may do it—without creating total havoc. I cannot decide to look after the ill, because I realize that if everyone were to look after the ill all the time, everything else would be neglected and no work would be done. If on the other hand no one looks after the ill, precisely because of this very consideration, the situation will be bad for the ill. We count in such cases on a division of labor.[4] We are, collectively, responsible to see to it that someone looks after the ill. But we are not obligated as individuals to do it ourselves, as long as there are enough people who will do it.

Now the responsibility over a shared memory is on each and every one in a community of memory to see to it that the memory will be kept. But it is not an obligation of each one to remember all. The responsibility to see to it that the memory is kept alive may require some minimal measure of memory by each in the community, but not more than that.

A Memory of Memory

Our notion of shared memory is based on the idea of a mnemonic division of labor. So far it has meant a synchronic division of labor, a division that takes place at a given point in time. But the idea of division of mnemonic labor can be extended diachronically as well. As a member of a certain community of memory, I am related to the memory of people from a previous generation. They in turn are related to the memory of people from the generation that preceded them, and so on, until we reach that generation which remembers the event in question first hand. This line of transition ends with a firsthand memory of a true event. That is, the first generation's memory of the episode, if true, means that the episode took place.

Indeed, personal memory, like personal knowledge, is an achievement. If it is true that I remember that the cat was on the mat eating bats, and likewise if it is true that I know that the cat was on the mat eating bats, then it is true that the cat was on the mat eating bats. On the other hand, if I merely believe that the cat was on the mat eating bats, it does not follow that the cat was on the mat eating bats.

However, while the personal use of *remember* is akin to *know* in the sense just explained, the collective use of *remember* is closer to *believe* than to *know*. Consider the Jews' shared memory of their Exodus from Egypt. Even if it is true that we have such a memory, it does not follow that that dramatic event ever occurred. A shared memory of a historical event that goes beyond the experience of anyone alive is a memory of memory, and not necessarily a memory that, through the division of diachronic labor, ends up at an actual event. This kind of memory reaches alleged memories of the past but not necessarily past events.

The last statement calls for clarification. To say of an imbecile that he is a half-wit does not mean that he is a wit cut into two. No more than saying Arnold Schwarzenegger is an intellectual dwarf means that he is an intellectual and that he is also a dwarf. Expressions like *half-wit* or *intellectual dwarf* are unbreakable compounds. They cannot be split into their constituents without changing their meaning. Now I take the expression "the-collective-memory-of-the-Exodus-from-Egypt" as such a compound, which means that we cannot infer from it that there was an event in history, the Exodus from Egypt, such that, through the transmission of shared memory, we remember it. A shared memory may end up back in history not with an event but with an event-story.

Belonging to a community of shared memory does not necessarily mean giving up on the idea that event-memories are memories of actual events. Even if the Exodus memory is indeed memory of a true historical event, it is a *closed memory* of the event: the only line of memory leading to this event is the one authorized by the tradition of the community as its canonical line of memory. Other historical lines to the original event may be tolerated and even welcomed as long as they confirm the version of the traditional memory, but they are prohibited if they contradict or conflict with the traditional line of shared memory.

History, critical history, differs from shared memory in

its reluctance to rely on closed memories, that is, in its commitment to looking for alternative lines that connect a past event to its present historical descriptions. In doing history, one makes an ontological commitment to securing the event which the memory is about; not so in the case of a traditional shared memory. Being a fundamentalist in a given tradition amounts to believing that the event-memories of that tradition are indeed memories of true past events. Being a traditionalist, on the other hand, amounts to suspending judgment as to the truthfulness of the tradition's event-memories. For the traditionalist, the memory itself matters a great deal, while its veracity counts for less.

I have already introduced, without warning, the idea of *tradition* into the idea of shared memory. Tradition is one form of shared memory, one in which the line transmitting a version from the past is sanctified, authorized, or even canonized in such a way that it is immune to challenges based on alternative historical lines. The paradigmatic shared memory I have in mind is the memory of an episode. But shared memory can be expressed in a *legacy*—that is, a memory of abstract things such as attitudes and principles—or in a *heritage*, which consists of concrete objects such as buildings and monuments.

Shared memory may be an expression of *nostalgia*. Nostalgia, I hasten to say, is an important element of communal memory. But it is not as innocent a trait as one might think. The tendency toward *kitsch* representations of the past is closely related to nostalgia. But then, what is so bad about kitsch apart from being an expression of bad taste? That is, what is morally wrong about kitsch and in particular nostalgic kitsch?

An essential element of nostalgia is sentimentality. And the trouble with sentimentality in certain situations is that it distorts reality in a particular way that has moral consequences. Nostalgia distorts the past by idealizing it. People, events, and objects from the past are presented as endowed with pure innocence. An attack on the nostalgic past is like an attack on the paradigmatic kitsch objects of crying children, smiling beggars, gloomy clowns, sleeping babies, and sad, brown-eyed dogs. Nostalgia can be a vehicle of great tenderness toward the past, but it can also be accompanied by a menacing feeling, when the shared memory of the past is kitsch.

My criticism is strictly confined to sentimentality. By no means is it directed toward sentiments about the past or sentiments in the past. Indeed, collective memory has a great deal to do with retaining the sensibility of the past and not just its sense. By sensibility I mean here the systematic way by which emotions were and are tied to the events remembered. What was it like to be part of or watch that event? The amazement and horror in watching

the collapse of the twin towers in New York, let alone being there, is the kernel of the memory of the collapse and
not a ketchup added on top of it.

Sensibilities are transmitted less by institutions and
more by the heightened language of articulated poets, as
well (or not so well) as by the gestures of inarticulate
parents who were "there," as conveyed to their sons and
daughters. This issue of sentiments and sensibilities with
regard to the past occupies Chapters 4 and 5 of this book.

Collective Memory and Myth

Memory is usually contrasted with history. The contrast is
somewhat like that between common sense and science.
Just as science is regarded as a systematic and critical common sense, so history is regarded as a systematic and critical collective memory. But collective memory is really
more akin to conventional wisdom than to common
sense. Altogether, the analogy does justice to collective
memory as a form of shared memory.

Modern shared memory is located between the push
and pull of two poles: history and myth. By myth I do not
mean just false beliefs about the past, which are invested
with symbolic meaning and charged with powerful emotion. And by history I do not mean mere plausible beliefs
about the past, which are cold and critical. By locating

memory between history and myth I do not just mean that memory is torn between seeking truth and seeking "noble" lies.

Shared memory is torn between two worldviews, which are manifested, in their pure forms, by science on the one hand and by myth on the other. The contrastive feature is the Weberian contrast between viewing the world as an enchanted place (myth) and viewing the world as a disenchanted place (critical history).[5]

Myth, as an embodiment of the enchanted worldview, is populated with wondrous animals, supernatural interventions in nature and history, heroes and gods, and heroes on the way to becoming gods: all charmed and charming in the literal sense of the word. The ontology of history, in contrast, may include bigger-than-life heroes in the metaphorical sense of the word, and charming people, also in the metaphorical sense, or even charismatic people who aspire to belong to the two worlds. But the two worldviews are committed to different ontologies, to different explanations, and to different notions of cause and effect.

The contrast between these two worlds is rendered as a sort of Gestalt switch which occurred in modern times, once people first became aware of the importance of life in the present and not in the past. The spell of the enchanted world is supposed to have vanished. Still, in the world as we know it today, the two worldviews coexist side by side; indeed, with some people the two dwell within the very same soul, switching back and forth from one to the other.

It would be quite silly of me to go on and address such vast and vague notions as myth and history, and memory in between. What I want to address is something more modest. I want to compare just one element running through these three enterprises of history, myth, and memory—the element of "bringing to life."

Bringing to Life

In *Idolatry*, Moshe Halbertal and I dealt with four senses of the expression *living myth*, with many overlaps among those senses.[6] In one sense, a myth lives within a community when members of the community believe the myth as a literal truth, as if it were a plain historical narrative with, say, supernatural beings interacting with humans, and so on. Another sense of a myth's being alive is when a community is deeply impressed by the mythical story, even if it is perceived as a "noble lie." By being deeply impressed I am thinking of the willingness of the members of the community to shape their lives in light of the myth. The Oedipus story apparently had this effect over the Greeks. The third sense of living myth is that it is primordially fresh, vital, full of energy, vivid to the imagination, and vivid in its images.

A myth is living if it plays a role in a ritual that intends to revivify events and heroes. It is this fourth sense of a living myth that interests me here. The myths of the dying gods Adonis, Tammuz, Dionysus, or, for the matter, Jesus meet such a description. As I said, not only dying gods may be revivified but events too. Thus, according to the Kabbalist reading of the Passover *seder*, this ritual is meant not just to commemorate the event of Exodus but to revivify it. Revivification is not resurrection; it brings the dead to life in essence but not in form. A living myth is a sacred story, then, connected with revivifying elements from the past. In a worldview which recognizes this possibility that the world is a mystery, the world is still an enchanted place—fraught with possibilities of encountering creatures and events that do not fit scientific ontology.

In a world in which two polar worldviews are competing, the pole of history may contain vivid and animated descriptions which "bring the past to life." But bringing-to-life in this sense is an attribute of the description, not of the reality described. In the disenchanted world of critical history, there is no backward causality. We cannot affect the past; we cannot undo the past, resurrect the past, or revivify the past. Only *descriptions* of the past can be altered, improved, or animated. The past itself, unlike its descriptions, cannot be brought back either in form or in essence.

When history is contrasted with memory, history is habitually labeled as cold, even lifeless, whereas memory can be vital, vivid, and alive. What this contrast means is that stories about the past that are shared by a community are as a rule more vivid, more concrete, and better connected with live experiences than is critical history. There is nothing remarkable about this claim, and all we have to do is to see if it is true. But I believe that shared memory as a cement for the community involves a far more ambitious sense of live memory, a sense not unlike the one involved in revivification through myth. And I am not talking of traditional societies, in which the notions of shared memory and of collective sacred stories, or myths, go hand in hand. I am talking about communities of memory that are supposed to have undergone the Gestalt switch from an enchanted worldview to a disenchanted one. In particular, I have in mind, secular modern nation-states.

I mentioned already the revivification rituals of mythic heroes, those in-between creatures who belong both to the world of mortals and to the world of immortals. The civic cult of the great men, enshrined in such institutions as the French Pantheon or inscribed in school textbooks (say of the Third Republic), is shaped, I submit, as a cult of immortality. The main idea is to elevate the name of those who made a name for themselves, the chosen few, and through reflected glory make the common people of their community shine too. Ceremonial as the civil cult of the great men is, it is still commemorative.

In the cult of the fallen soldiers, as highlighted after World War I, the shared memory of the battlefields and the ritual attached to them contain strong elements of revivification. Those rituals are modeled on religious rituals. "In the night of Christmas the dead are conversing with human voices," writes Walter Plex, one of the architects of the shared memory of World War I.[7] The revivification takes the form of the living assuming the roles of their fallen comrades, as captured in the final stanza of John McCrae's "In Flanders Fields" (1915):

> Take up our quarrel with the foe:
> To you from failing hands we throw
> The torch; be yours to hold it high.
> If ye break faith with us who die
> We shall not sleep, though poppies grow
> In Flanders fields.

This is understood not as a mere act of identification but as an act of true identity.

One can discern two moves in shaping the cult of the fallen soldiers: one is to create, metaphorically speaking, a high-energy situation that can bring about a fusion of the two opposing categories of life and death, where the dead continue to participate actively in the redemptive war. The second move is that of cooling the accelerator after the war, by fusing and confusing the two categories of commemoration and revivification. What is brought to life in successful commemoration is memory, whereas in revivification the believers have the idea that the dead are brought to life, not in form but in essence.

What does the power, or rather the illusion of power, to bring to life by collective memory amount to? I believe that it amounts to a great deal. It strongly indicates that a community of memory is a community based not only on actual thick relations to the living but also on thick relations to the dead. It is a community that deals with life and death, where the element of commemoration verging on revivification is stronger than in a community based merely on communication. It is a community that is concerned with the issue of survival through memory.

Communities of Memory

Natural communities of memory are families, clans, tribes, religious communities, and nations. There is of course nothing natural about shared memory, and nothing natural about the groups that are the natural candidates for being communities of memory—if by natural we mean natural kinds. They are all, in the jargon of today, social constructs. However, if the contrast between a social construct and a natural kind has to do with the idea that a social construct is changeable while a natural kind is immutably fixed by its essence, then it is a contrast ill understood. After all, it is on the whole much easier to change and manipulate the genetic makeup of natural kinds like ducks and daffodils than to change such social constructs as the Dutch language or delinquent behavior. The outcome of a change in a natural kind is a new natural kind. This is a deep metaphysical point. But from an anthropological point of view we may still treat the new changed natural kind as we treated the old kind. More importantly, from an anthropological point of view, social habits and institutions are on the whole more resilient under the pressure of change than the essences of natural kinds.

In talking about natural candidates for communities of memory I mentioned groups that, left on their own, are very likely to become communities of memory, usually quite spontaneously and sometimes with the help of manipulation. Thus, it has been noted that the agrarian middle-class peasants, the so-called kulaks, who were "liquidated" on Stalin's orders in 1929, did not constitute a community of memory. As a response to the revolution of

1905, this agrarian middle class came about through a deliberate effort of the czarist regime to create a class of loyalists among the peasants by making them owners of middle-sized farms. It is easier to create a class with common economic interests than with a shared memory.

Against the background of the question, Who will remember the murdered Kulaks and who should remember them? I wish to raise two further questions: First, why cannot the kulaks be remembered by humanity at large? That is, why cannot humanity be shaped into a community of memory and why cannot it be formed into an ethical community, based on the thick relation of caring? And second, should not the kulaks be remembered by humanity even if humanity is regarded, in my terms, as a moral community? Ought not this moral community to have some minimal sense of memory for, say, the Gulags, the kulaks, Majdanek and Treblinka, Hiroshima and Nanking, as warning signposts in human moral history?

The first question I shall view from the perspective of two religious projects which, for lack of better labels, I shall call the Christian project and the Jewish project. The Christian project is an effort to establish, in historical time, an ethical community based on love. This community, ideally, should include all of humanity, and it should be based on the memory of the cross as an ultimate sacrifice for the sake of humanity. The memory of what led to

THE ETHICS OF MEMORY

the cross is brought to life either by a sacramental act of revivification (among Catholics) or by commemoration (among Protestants). The idea in both cases, however, is that, with a little helping of grace, humanity can and should be established as an ethical community of love.

The Jewish project retains the double tier of ethics and morality at least for historical times, and postpones the idea of a universal ethical community to the messianic era. Jews are obligated to establish themselves as an ethical community of caring. The force of the obligation is gratitude to God for having delivered their ancestors from the "house of slaves" in Egypt. The crucial role of memory for the Jewish community is to serve as a constant reminder of this debt of gratitude. In distinction from ethics, morality, in the Jewish view, is based on a different source. It is based on the debt of gratitude all of humanity owes God for having been created in His image. (I find it interesting that the term used in the Koran for the infidel, *kafir*, was used originally to mean ingratitude, a use that can be found in the Koran itself.)

The two projects have a common feature. They both base their obligation on a debt of gratitude that should be kept in memory. The memories for which we ought to be grateful are positive memories: creation, the sacrifice on the cross, Exodus. These are memories of divine gifts to humanity, or, in the case of Exodus, to the Jews. In contrast, the candidates for memory in the case of humanity as a moral community are negative ones, mostly of terrible acts of cruelty. Such memories do not inspire gratitude. Instead, they ignite an appetite for revenge.

Caring, is, I believe, at the center of our ethical relations, not gratitude. We owe each other two different kinds of things in ethics and morality: in morality, human respect; in ethics, caring and loyalty. So in my account, Scanlon's formula of "what we owe each other" does not encapsulate both morality and ethics, for we owe two different things under that formula.[8] This idea of deep gratitude, and especially the horror of ingratitude as in the case of betrayal, is what we get from the religious account of ethics and morality as based on gratitude to God.

Be that as it may be, between the brother and the other there is room for many possible projects beyond the two religious projects, projects which do not find much room for memories, whether moral or ethical. The project advanced by Peter Kropotkin, Russia's primary proponent of anarchism, turns all others into brothers once the corrupting forces of the state are removed and our instinctive fraternity takes hold.[9] Julia Kristeva's project turns all brothers into others, which means no thick relations at all.[10] Unlike the two religious projects, these two secular projects differ from one another even as they share a common assumption: namely, that no gratitude should be felt toward the past and there is no room for a community of memory.

For Kropotkin, an instinctive sense of mutual aid, rather than shared memory, cements his futuristic community. He would deny the moral force of remembering crimes against humanity because the conditions for forming his ideal community are such that all crimes against humanity will end. In Kristeva's celebration of otherness, instead of fixed identities and a stable society we have a carnival of changing masks at will. The idea of shared memories of whatever kind is positively harmful here. It is an oppressive instrument in fixing identities—national, religious, or what have you.

A Universal Ethical Community

Two questions emerge with regard to the project of establishing a universal ethical community. (1) Is it feasible? (2) Is it desirable?

We may say with the counter-Enlightenment thinker G. K. Chesterton, the father of the old private eye Father Brown, that the trouble with the Christian project of transforming humanity into a community of love is not that it has been tried and found wanting but that it has been left untried. But then, why not try it? Perhaps it should be tried without religious trappings, which are local and parochial even when they attempt to speak to humanity at large.

Why is it so difficult to shape humanity into an ethical community? True, it is an imagined community, the farthest of all possible communities from being based on face-to-face relations. But then face-to-face relations of acquaintance are neither necessary nor sufficient for caring, as the cement of an ethical community. The child who cares about his mother whom he has never seen shows that they are not necessary, and the priest and Levite from the story of the Good Samaritan show that they are not sufficient.

In short, we may care for people and for communities we have not encountered nor are likely to encounter in our lifetime. So why should not humanity constitute such a community based on caring? The attitude of caring, after all, is based on belonging, not on achievement. So belonging to the "family of man" should be enough. What do we imagine when we imagine a community with whom we are supposed to have thick relations? My answer is that we imagine an extension of family relations that would include relatives we have not met. So why not imagine "the family of man" to be such an extended family?

The issue is whether caring, as the cement of an ethical community, can hold without any *contrast*. Is it meaningful to have friends if we have no foes? And if such a contrast is necessary, then, so the argument goes, humanity cannot provide the contrast, since it is the most extensive community imaginable and there is nothing and nobody relevant outside of that community to be contrasted with. Caring might turn into a pale, meaningless notion. If contrastless caring is a conceptual impossibility, then the idea of transforming humanity into an ethical community of caring is itself logically impossible, and not just hard to achieve empirically. Moreover, from the fact that some imagined communities are ethical communities it does not follow that humankind, as a whole, can be such a community.

If, on the other hand, we think about a nation as a paradigmatic ethical community of the modern era, then the contrast is very pronounced. A nation has famously been defined as a society that nourishes a common delusion about its ancestry and shares a common hatred for its neighbors. Thus, the bond of caring in a nation hinges on false memory (delusion) and hatred of those who do not belong.

To be sure, there is no scarcity in stories of a common origin for the human community, be it Adam and Eve in the monotheistic religions or the first pair of naked apes in evolutionary theory. This latter view about the origin of humanity is much better established and less delusional than the myth of origin of most nations. But the second element, hatred, is disturbing, since we recognize the truth in it. I choose my words advisedly: not the truth *of* it, but the truth *in* it. Namely, it is a historical fact that the bond of solidarity in many nations depends to a considerable extent on hatred, whether active or platonic, of the nation's neighbor.

What is the nature of the contrast needed, if indeed it is needed, for the relation of caring to make sense? The nature of the contrast is the question, whether it is a conceptual contrast, as between consonant and vowel, or a mere psychological contrast.

But even if the notion of caring conceptually requires a contrast, the required contrast need not actually exist so long as we can *envisage* those who are not cared for. If the concept of darkness conceptually needs light as its contrast, it is still possible to talk about darkness, as in the book of Genesis, "upon the face of the deep" before the creation of light, if light is a possibility. So, if conceptual contrast does not require actual contrast, then transforming humanity into an ethical community of caring and of shared memory is not a conceptual impossibility.

Still, such a transformation is very difficult to achieve. This does not mean that we should give up on the regulative idea of the human commonwealth as an ethical community of caring. But it does mean that in the meantime we should aim for a second best, that is, turning humanity into a *moral* community. Now I am, in general, more interested in what will make things better than in what will make things best. So let me turn to the question of whether humanity, as a moral community, ought to have some minimal shared moral memories, or whether the business of memory should be left entirely to smaller ethical communities.

On the face of it, there are things humanity at large ought to remember. When Hitler asked, "Who today remembers the Armenians?" the resounding answer should have been, "We all do." Or, at least, "The enlightened world does." (The irony in Hitler's question is that in fact he counted on his listeners to remember the Armenians. The irony escaped me and was pointed out to me by Peter Pulzer.) So what should humanity remember? The short answer is: striking examples of radical evil and crimes against humanity, such as enslavement, deportations of civilian populations, and mass exterminations.

Radical evil as an act perpetrated for the sole reason that "it is evil" is not a coherent idea. This in any case is what I believe Kant believed. Even Satan cannot, conceptually, act for the reason that it is the evil thing to do. Milton's Arch-Fiend says "ever doing ill our sole delight," but even he does it not for the sake of evil but as a rebellious act, to oppose the high will of God.[11] However, there is still the notion that Kant's call is for radical evil. I borrow from Kant the expression, not the explanation, of "radical evil."[12]

Radical evil consists, I suggest, of acts that undermine the very foundation of morality itself. Nazi eliminative biologism, as exercised in the elimination of Jews and Gypsies as subhuman, was a direct onslaught on the very idea of shared humanity. Hence, it was a direct onslaught on morality itself. Such an attack on morality should be recorded and remembered. And with it, gross crimes against humanity that undercut the root of morality, that is, shared humanity; hence my use of the adjective *radical*, the Latin for *root*.

But even if such a thin notion of memory shared by the whole of mankind is desirable and important, the politics of constructing this memory is immeasurably difficult. It is hard to form effective institutions that will store such memories and diffuse them. Such institutions are likely to be bureaucratic and soulless. Memory is too tied to the idea of immortality to expect that anonymous humanity can serve as a community of commemoration when it fails miserably as a community of communication.

What is more, shared memory depends not just on a network of people and organizations to carry out the division of mnemonic labor but also on the remembered items themselves belonging to coherent networks. It is hard to carry the memory of isolated and unconnected events and people, taken from very different histories. To remember, say, the massacres in My Lai or in Dir Yasin as isolated items in the Vietnam war and Israel's war of independence does not amount to much.

An additional problem is the danger of biased salience. Events from the so-called First World, or the technologically developed world, are likely to be more salient to us than comparable events in the Third World. Thus, our memory of Kosovo overshadows our memory of Rwanda. Moreover, because they are likely to be better remembered, the atrocities of Europe will come to be perceived as morally more significant than atrocities elsewhere. As such, they claim false moral superiority. The situation is like that of the proverbial colonial student who boasted to his compatriot, "I flunked in Oxford whereas you only flunked at the London School of Economics." There is snobbism in failure, not just in success.

These are some of my worries with regard to the project of constructing a shared moral memory for mankind. All in all I am unclear in my mind as to how to go about creating such a memory. But I am pretty clear about how not to go about it.

We are, I guess, all familiar by now with one of the well-intentioned proposals to shape the much debated Holocaust memorial monument in Berlin with the biblical

commandment "Thou shall not kill." Though this suggestion, by using the Hebrew script and words of the biblical
commandment, makes a faint gesture toward the fact that
the victims were overwhelmingly Jewish, still the message
of this suggestion is unmistakable: the monument in Berlin is being erected by humanity, for humanity.

The way I see it, this suggestion makes two blunders.
One, the standing of the Germans as a community of
memory connected to the perpetrators does not leave
them the option of acting on behalf of humanity at large.
They are a side to this memory. Moreover, there is something wrong in depicting the victims under the mere label
of "human beings," when it is clear that many of them, especially the East Europeans, would have identified themselves as Jews. So even if one strongly advocates the project of constructing a monument of shared memory for all
of mankind, it is wrong for the Germans to do it, all the
more so in Berlin.

The monument in Berlin, as I view it, should be an effort by the German people to reestablish themselves as
an ethical community, encumbered with painful shared
memories. The way for the Germans to reestablish themselves as an ethical community is to turn their cruelty,
which was what tied them to the Jews, into repentance.

With all due differences, the same holds with regard
to the Japanese community vis-à-vis the Korean comfort

women. To include these women in the Japanese shared memory is to bring them to life by recognizing their suffering, and that is the first step toward repentance.

I still believe that the most promising projects of shared memory are those that go through natural communities of memory, so to speak, and the issue is how to engage painful traumatic memories from the past. This I believe is not as utopian as the two universalistic projects I mentioned, mankind as an ethical community or mankind as a moral community of memory. Even the project of remembering the gloomiest of memories is a hopeful project. It ultimately rejects the pessimist thought that all will be forgotten, as expressed by Ecclesiastes: "There is no remembrance of former things, nor will there be any remembrance of things that are to come amongst those who shall come after" (1:11). The project of memory is not vanity of vanities.

Why ought humanity to remember moral nightmares rather than moments of human triumph—moments in which human beings behaved nobly? Of course there is something good and endearing in us humans all over the world remembering such glorious events and the people who were involved in them. But the issue for us to sort out is what humanity *ought* to remember rather than what is good for humanity to remember. There is asymmetry between protecting morality and promoting it. Promoting is highly desirable. Protecting is a must.

The source of the obligation to remember, I maintain, comes from the effort of radical evil forces to undermine morality itself by, among other means, rewriting the past and controlling collective memory.

3

THE KERNEL

Ethical Assessment

ARE THERE things that we ought to remember? This is still our question. I shall try to distill an answer, based on the discussion of the previous two chapters.

The first stage in my distillation is to give more of an account of what is involved in ethics and in ethical assessments. The second stage is to give more of an account of how our attitude toward leaving traces after death is a good test of the meaning of memory for our thick relations, and thereby for the ethical demand to remember. The third stage in the distillation is to give more of an account of a community of memory and its relation to the national memory. Only then will my distilled answer emerge.

The concern of ethics is thick relationships among people, relations that call for actions. My claim is that the reasons for ethical actions are grounded in the thick relations themselves, and not in the properties of those who are involved in the relations. "I help her because she is my daughter." This reason fully justifies, ethically, my helping her. Such reasons are of course defeasible, that is, they can in principle be defeated. (Had my daughter treated me as wretchedly as Father Goriot's daughters did in Balzac's celebrated novel, I might reconsider my reason as well as my actions.)

In my account of ethics, *good* and *bad* are to be directly attributed to relationships. For example, a sadomasochistic relation is bad, whereas mother-daughter relations are good. But then why are mother-daughter relations good? For two reasons, positive and negative. The positive reason: mother-daughter relations are caring relations. The negative reason: those relations do not violate moral demands. There is, however, a need to distinguish between good and bad *within* the relation and goodness and badness *of* the relation. In saying that the mother-daughter relation is good, we are talking about the goodness *of* the relation. But we are sorely aware that such good relations can turn sour and become bad relations. When this happens, however, it is badness *within* the relation, not the badness *of* the relation.

But then what makes for the badness *of* the relationship of sadomasochism? One answer is humiliation. But if humiliation is what makes it bad, then it seems that sadomasochistic relations are bad on moral grounds, not on ethical grounds. Humiliation in the strong sense, by its very definition, hurts the victim's human dignity, and the attribute of human dignity is, in my division of labor, the concern of morality, not of ethics.[1] Hence the inference that sadomasochism is bad on moral grounds, not on ethical grounds.

Well, I maintain that morality is indeed a basis for disqualifying ethical relations. Ethical relations are bad relations if they are immoral. Morality provides a threshold test for the assessment of ethical relations. But the sufficiency condition for making an ethical relation a *good* ethical relation is caring. Caring is the ethical contribution to the goodness of the relation. Sadomasochism does not pass the threshold test. Also, it is not a caring relation: the sadist who finds his gratification in inflicting pain and degradation takes pleasure in cruelty, not in caring.

Ethical relations cannot be immoral, then. Still, there is need for a distinction between the immorality of those involved in the relation and the immorality of the relation itself. Good ethical relations can hold among immoral people. It is just not true that only the "charming night," in Baudelaire's phrase, is the friend of the criminal. Criminals are capable of good friendships in the two senses of good—goodness *of* the relation and goodness *within* the relation. But ethical relations as such cannot be immoral relations: exploitative, demeaning, cruel, humiliating, and so on. Sadomasochism does not qualify as an ethical relation, and there is no point in calling it a bad ethical relation since it is not ethical to begin with. The situation here is not unlike the ambiguity we face in aesthetics between saying that a given piece is "not sculpture" and that it is "bad sculpture."

But strictly speaking, sadomasochism, in my account, is not an ethical relation. So what are we to consider as an example of a bad ethical relation? Treating your children morally but in a way that is indistinguishable from the way you treat strangers is an example of a bad ethical relation. It is moral, but bad. Ethically bad that is.

Ethical relations involve partiality—that is, favoring a person or a group over others with equal moral claim. So how can we require ethical relations to pass the morality threshold test? Is, for example, nepotism—that is, favoritism based on family ties—unethical? If it is, then what kind of partiality is allowed?

Ethical relations are allowed to be partial as a moral tiebreaker but not otherwise. Take the case where a man sees two strangers on the verge of drowning, and he can save only one. This man has a very strong moral reason to save the life of one of them, but he has no moral reason to save the life of one rather than the other. The rescuer faces a situation of picking, not of choosing, between the two.[2] Choosing is always selecting for a reason. In picking, you have only a reason to make some choice or other; but no particular reason to make the specific choice you do. This situation of picking is similar to facing a shelf in the supermarket that has identical cans of soup. You have a reason to select one, but not a reason for the particular one that you pick. Picking and choosing can go for the big and the small, saving a life or buying soup.

Whomever the rescuer saves, he does it by picking him, not by choosing him. Now let us change the situation to fit the proverbial case in which one of the persons on the verge of drowning is the man's wife and the other is a stranger. The two in danger have equal moral claim to be saved. But in this case the man is not supposed to pick; he is required to chose. The requirement is not moral, since the two people in danger are in a moral tie. The blood of the one is not redder than the blood of the other; both have an equal moral right to life. The requirement is rather ethical. For the husband to be impartial, he would have to approach the problems as though he were facing two strangers. His obligation, however, is not to be impartial. Picking between the two, rather than choosing his wife, might be justifiable, but it would be ethically cursed. Ethics requires partiality in this case of a moral tie.

Nepotism, on the other hand, is not a case of breaking a moral tie or a near moral tie; it is favoring a family member over a nonmember who has a much better moral claim to the job or position. Nepotism is not a tiebreaker; it is immoral and unethical.

How objective is the ethical assessment of a relation? An ethical assessment of a relation as good or bad is open not just to those involved in the relation. It is not only the first-person perspective of the one who acts on reasons grounded in the relation, say the lover, who is capable of making an ethical assessment. Nor is it only the second-person perspective of the loved one who is capable of making the ethical assessment. It should in principle be open to the third-person perspective of any bystander as well. This applies as far as the goodness or badness *of* the relation is concerned.

But then what about having a third person judging the badness *in* the relation? Isn't this a case that calls specifically only to the one involved in the relation to judge? No. A third person is fully capable of judging the badness *in* the relation, assuming that the third person takes into account how the relation looks to the people involved. Indeed, it is essential to assessing the goodness or badness *in* a relation for the third person to see how the relations are viewed from within.

If we regard a third-person perspective as an objective perspective, then ethics is objective. But we should be wary of one sense of objective, which I deem a threat to ethics. It is the sense of objective that strongly suggests mind-independent, thing-like objects. Viewing human relations as thing-like objects is a mistake. It masks the very nature of ethics as dealing with human relations.

One objection to the idea of grounding ethics in relations rather than in the properties of the individual (such as rationality) is that feudal ethics was romantically characterized in terms of personal relations. It took many years and a great deal of effort—from no lesser a thinker than Kant himself—to counter feudal ethics. There was a strong need to anchor morality not on personal relations but on making each person an autonomous human being. Autonomy is characterized by properties rather than by relations. Or to put it more accurately, autonomy is couched in one-place predicates ("being rational"), whereas feudal ethics is couched on multi-place predicates ("being a vassal of . . .").

My objection to feudal ethics is not how many places its predicates take but the kind of relations it consists of. Feudal ethics is based on bad relations, that is, on inherently exploitative relations. These are bad relations in the strong sense—that is, the badness *of* the relations. In any case, we should not throw the baby out with the bath water—the baby being ethics based on good, thick relations, and the bath water being feudal ethics based on bad relations.

There is an intriguing twist to this last point, concerning religious ethics. Is religious ethics of the familiar kind, with its feudal-like Lord demanding total submission, a feudal ethics, or is it rather an ethical system based on loving fatherly care? This is a good question to ask, but not now and not here.

Memory and Death

Now to the second stage of the distillation, which has to do with the relation between memory and our attitude toward death.

We dread the idea of dying without leaving a trace. "Speak for yourself," you might say. But even without research I believe that I speak for many. Some of us understand this yearning for traces as a substitute for the yearning for the afterlife. The yearning for an afterlife is what religion captures. While the yearning for an afterlife is understandable, the belief in it is not. For one thing, it is not clear what it can mean and whether what it supposedly means—reconstitution in body and soul—is at all coherent. The issue here is not the truth of the belief but its very meaning.

So the problem is how to devise a notion of a trace that does not commit us to a metaphysical belief in an afterlife but still satisfies our yearning to avoid oblivion. One candidate is being remembered after our death, at least by those we care about. This is a flimsy notion of an after-life—living on the lips of others, as it were. The prospects for living on others' lips after our death are much better than for having a full-fledged afterlife in body and soul (whatever that's supposed to mean). Living on others' lips is just a fanciful metaphor for the humdrum reality that people might go on talking about us and mentioning us after our death. There is nothing mysterious in this mode of existence, as compared with other forms of afterlife. But then the question is how realistic is it to expect to be re-membered and to be talked about after our death? This is a disappointing substitute for our yearning for afterlife. But it is the only thing that we can rationally entertain, and even that is too much to ask, as I shall argue shortly.

There are some who make a name for themselves. They can rest assured that they are going to lead a glorious afterlife on others' lips as well as writing. This, after all, is what glory means. But what about the rest of us, whose or-dinary lives leave nothing in particular for future genera-tions to talk about? What can we rationally hope for in terms of being remembered after our death? We may get a glimpse of the answer by asking ourselves how many branches we can climb on our own family tree. Grandfa-ther? Great grandmother? For most of us this is as much as we can remember. So our prospects of being remem-bered after our death are not terribly promising, if by "after" we mean something like more than fifty years after. Even this faint substitute for the grand religious promise of being reconstituted in body and soul is far from being secured.

In asking how realistic are our expectations of being remembered, I took the question as if it were about predicting the future. Namely, what degree of credence can we ascribe to the belief that we will be remembered in the future? But a better sense of expectation is the normative sense. To say that I expect you to remember me is to say that you *should* remember me, if our relations now are as thick as I believe them to be. This is not a prediction but a prescription. We address such normative expectations to those with whom we have thick personal relations. They offer a basis for rational hope; there is nothing outlandish in the expectation of being remembered by those to whom we matter during our life. So the main thrust of my expectation is not the predictive thrust but the normative thrust. I expect them to remember not in a sense that they necessarily will but that they should, because of the thickness of our relations. The expectation to be remembered is in this sense an evaluation of the intensity and quality of our thick relations now, while we are still around.

We want to have the kind of intense relations that will deserve to go on after our death. We want to be remembered by those who survive us and who used to care for us as we cared for them while we were still alive. We would like to have the kind of relations that make an impact on their lives, and this is the meaning of leaving traces. The horror of falling into utter oblivion is not necessarily the fear of what will happen to us after death but of what it says about our relationships now. It is the fear of not amounting to much in our present relations with others.

So in caring about leaving traces and being remembered we rationally care about our thick relations and their endurance. This is what we are allowed to hope for in terms of leaving traces. Does this meet the yearning of many people for the afterlife? It probably does not. Does this meet the yearning for personal glory? I am afraid the answer again is no. But this is all we can rationally hope for: to be remembered by those with whom we maintain thick relations.

All this, if true, seems to hold with regard to personal relations. We expect our near and dear to remember us. But what can we hope for from collective memory? Will the community remember us? *Should* the community remember us? By "us" I mean ordinary individuals. These questions bring us to the third stage in the distillation.

Hopes from a Community of Memory

In saying that we expect those with whom we have close, dense, meaningful relations to remember us, we are not restricted to those with whom we have face-to-face relations. True, we cannot learn to swim by correspondence, but we may form deep friendship by correspondence without having face-to-face relations. One may even love God on the strength of His letters sent via his postmen, the prophets.

The possibility of forming epistolary friendships is very much to the point here. It indicates that our thick relations may have a strong notional element. Notional does not mean fictional. My own imagined community, the Jewish people, although a very complicated community to imagine, is not fiction. There is such a collective, which supervenes on individuals who interact causally. In contrast, my love of Jane Austen's imagined heroine Elizabeth Bennett is a love of a fictional character. Elizabeth Bennett's written description causally interacts with me, but there is no Elizabeth Bennett to so interact.

It is a remarkable feature of human beings, symbolic animals that we are, that we can form symbolic bonds and not just face-to-face attachments. Packs of wolves and prides of lions are related only by face-to-face attachments based on licking and smelling. We human beings can do better, and lead collective existences based on symbols that encapsulate shared memories. Collective existences are webs of relations based on bonds in which shared memories play a crucial role.

So do we expect our community of memory to remember us after we are dead? We do not expect to be remembered individually by the nation. But many of us are so woven into the web of thick national relations that the use of the first-person plural "we" is quite natural. This "we" is an enduring body that will survive after our personal death. We shall not be remembered personally, but we shall be remembered by taking part in events that will be remembered for their significance in the life of the collective.

One may accept the idea of thick ethical relations based on personal relations but still find the idea of thick collective relations an illusion. Thus Russell Hardin, a keen connoisseur of claims for group identity, writes sarcastically: "Indeed, many writers even give credit to some notion of collective memory that connects, say, contemporary Serbs with the dreadfully lost war with the Turks in 1389 in the Field of the Blackbirds. Somehow, the English seem to be exempt from the effects of the dreadful memories of Hastings Field." And he goes on to remark that "the assertion of historical memory contributes to mystification rather than explanation or understanding."[3]

I for one belong to "the many writers" who give credit to the notion of collective memory. Moreover, I believe that there is a connection between the contemporary Serbs and the battle of Kosovo (the Blackbirds) in 1389. Indeed, it is a good question to ask why the Serbs remember vividly the battle of 1389. Why is it that Serb jingoists can stir things up merely by writing the number "1389" on walls? It is also a good question to ask why writing the number "1066" on the walls in York would look incomprehensible, even if the people in York knew that this is the date of the Battle of Hastings. Both are good questions, and there is no mystery in what would count as good answers to them. The meaning of the two events is very different for the two communities involved. Calling both battles "dreadful defeats" and asking why one dreadful defeat is remembered and the other is forgotten does not even begin to provide an understanding of what goes into the memory of these events.

The Battle of Hastings was more a war of succession to the crown of a childless king than a conquest by an alien force—much like the ascension of William of Orange to the throne in 1688. Besides, mostly good things happened in England after the battle: better institutions, more law and order, and an end to internal strife. So no wonder that not much bad blood and not many dreadful memories remain from that battle. Even the battle itself ended inconclusively, and only the killing of Harold turned it into a Norman victory. There was, in short, no dreadful defeat in Hastings.

The defeat of the Serbs in Kosovo, though heroic, was dreadful indeed. It meant something very different for the

Serbs than Hastings meant for the English. It marked the fall of a glorious Serbian independent state, and—after the second defeat in Kosovo—the inception of a vassal state for four hundred years under the Ottomans, an alien force with a different religion. There is also no mystery as to how the memory of this event was kept alive among the Serbs. The Ottomans allowed only one Serbian national institution to survive, the Serbian Orthodox Church. It was a national church created by the deposed Dushan dynasty. A national church is a powerful agent of collective memory, and it was the church as a community of memory that kept the memory of the Kosovo battle alive.

True, the Macbethian couple Slobodan and Mirjana Milosevic cynically exploited and manipulated the memory of Kosovo in order to galvanize Serbian support for their rule. But the couple did not invent the battle of Kosovo, nor did they create its memory among the Serbs. If there is something that I find mysterious it is the immense power accredited by some writers to the elites, who supposedly manipulate the masses by inventing communal stories to promote their own selfish interests. What I find even more puzzling is why members of the elite, who according to this account are supposed to know so well the nature of the manipulation, are willing to send their own sons to get killed in national wars? Does endangering their own enlisted sons serve their interests? More often than not, elites put a spin on collective memories because they believe in them. They believe that their story is basically sound and all they do is give it some color to make it more evocative.

The question is not whether collective memory is manipulated. It usually is. The interesting question to ask is why the manipulators choose to manipulate national memories and not, say, class memories. Why did Stalin, an arch-manipulator, when locked in a war of life and death with the invading Nazis, invoke the national memories of great patriots from czarist Russia rather than working-class memories that he was ideologically supposed to represent? Stalin invoked the memory of Alexander Nevsky, who defeated the Teutonic knights (in the thirteenth century), rather than the memory of Karl Marx, and of Ivan the Terrible, who defeated the Tartars at Kazan in the sixteenth century, rather than Friedrich Engles. The distinction needed, once again, is between the illusion *of a* collective memory and illusions *within* the collective memory. There may be illusions within collective memory, but it is wrong to infer from that to the illusion *of* collective memory.

National collectivism, even if real, is for the critic nothing but a secular substitute for the religious idea of an afterlife, and a rather shabby substitute at that. Being one with the nation is a shabby idea in the sense in which immortality without individuality is. Religion at least makes the big promise of individual survival. But why should I care if my soul "cleaves to eternal truth," thus gaining the immortality of the eternal truth, or "becomes one with one of the spheres above the moon"? In the same spirit we can ask, Why should I care if my soul is swallowed up by a collective? It is like a drop of water, which tries to gain salvation by merging with the ocean, thereby losing its identity as a drop without adding much to the ocean. It is even worse. Far from shabby, eternal truths, like the truths of mathematics, have great nobility to them, whereas with nationalism and tribalism it is shabbiness all the way down. Or so says the critic.

I shall try to avoid the question whether nationalism is good or bad. Nationalism can be good and nationalism can be bad. This in itself is a good indication that the issue is the badness *within* the relations that comprise nationalism, and not the badness *of* the relations. It takes one cockroach found in your food to turn the most otherwise delicious meal into a bad experience. (I owe this analogy to Paul Rozin.) It takes 30 to 40 ethnic groups who are fighting one another to make the 1,500 or more significant ethnic groups in the world who live more or less peacefully look bad. In any case, the social unit for my discussion of collective memory and of our obligation to have shared memory is not necessarily the nation, the ethnic group, or, for that matter, the tribe, but instead it is the community of memory—whatever it happens to be.

The relation between a community of memory and a nation is such that a proper community of memory may help shape a nation, rather than the nation shaping the community of memory. A nation is a natural candidate for forming a community of memory not because of the temporal priority of the nation. It is in the contents of the shared memories, such as a common origin or a shared past, that nations are interested in.

But there are other ways to shape communities of memory. And some of these communities are not less effective than the nation as memory entrepreneurs in drawing attention to the memory of their members. About 3,000 people were murdered in New York City on September 11. About 300 of them were firemen. There has been a great deal of commemoration in the city since September, but without question the commemoration and the attention have been very unevenly distributed among the victims. In saying "unevenly" I do not wish to imply that the memory was unjustly distributed. I wish to merely state the fact that the firemen who died in the rescue effort have received overwhelming attention in comparison with all other victims.

There are many reasons why this is so. The obvious reason is the heroism of these people, who put their own lives at risk to save others. Heroes are always venerated and remembered more extensively than ordinary people are. This holds true even in egalitarian societies. But there is also a less obvious reason for the uneven distribution of attention. The firefighters were thickly related to various communities of memory in ways that other victims were not. Many of them were Irish Catholic and Italian Catholic with parishes and priests of their own. They belonged to a professional association that is the closest thing in the modern world to a medieval guild. The guild, with its ritualistic fraternity, contributes greatly to keeping the memory of firefighters alive. The guild has its memory entrepreneurs who are good at drawing public attention. They made sure, for example, that Mayor Rudy Giuliani, with his outstanding visibility, did not skip any of their memorial services, thus making him the father figure of their densely related fraternity.

I use the example of the firefighter guild as a reminder that communities of memory take many forms, even in a cosmopolitan city like New York. We should not be stuck with one stock example of the nation as the only possible community of memory.

There is, however, something more specific to say here about suitable candidates for forming ethical communities of memory. Our ethical relations seem like natural extensions of family relations. By claiming that family relations are the basis of ethical relations I mean that the formative metaphor for thick ethical relations are familial relations. The fraternity of a guild is a metaphorical extension of brotherly relations, as the term *fraternity* suggests. Thick family relations lend themselves to phony metaphorical extensions. Heads of soulless corporations love to talk to their employees as "one big family." This is a cheap and hollow device for mustering loyalty by invoking the name of the family in vain.

The true issue in assessing national relations in ethical terms is whether or not, in claiming to be an extended family, they are a natural extension of the family metaphor. Not all nations pretend to be "organic nations" with a shared myth of common origin, but those that do should be ethically scrutinized as to whether their purported thick relations are sufficiently family-like. The scrutiny involves a great deal of factual claims and should be done on a retail basis, case by case. The resemblance to the family tests whether the relation is really thick.

Then and only then should we ask if these relations are also good relations, and not just thick ones. In the case of the nation we should ask to what an extent national ties among members hinge on hatred of the outside world: Do you actually need a foe in order to have a compatriot friend? The family metaphor can go in many directions. In one direction it can stress the element of common descent, as "organic" nations do. Or it can completely ignore that element and stress instead brotherly relations tested in trying times, as in the case of the firemen guild.

The family metaphor as the formative metaphor for thick relations may one day lose its grip. In a society where half of all marriages dissolve in divorce, this metaphor may be seriously eroded and other forms of thick relations, like friendships, may in the future become paradigmatic. Indeed, both David Hume and Adam Smith nominated friendship as the formative metaphor for thick relations in a "commerce society" (read "market economy"), rather than family relations. For one thing, we choose our friends, while we do not choose our parents. And free choice is at the center of liberal society.[4]

The competition between the two formative metaphors—family and friends—for collective thick relations is important. But no matter how the competition will be resolved, the family is still with us. The very insistence of the gay community on having their marriage ("civil union") recognized by law, without being satisfied with friendship as a substitute, makes me think that the family metaphor of thick relations still retains its hold.

The Distilled Answer

After the three stages of distillation, it is time for a distilled answer to the question whether there are things that we ought to remember. First, how should we understand the *ought* in the ethical context? I think that the ethical *ought* should be used in a sense akin to *medical ought*. Medical ought-to, as in "you ought to avoid eating fat," "you ought to exercise," "you ought to take your medicine," is relative to the assumption that you want to be healthy. There is no obligation to be healthy. But if you want to be healthy, this is what it takes. There is no obligation, in my view, to be engaged in ethical relations. It remains an option to lead a polite solitary life with no engagements and no commitments of the sort involved in ethical life. The *ought* of morality, on the other hand, is different from the *ought* in ethics. Being moral is a required good; being ethical is, in principle, an optional good. The stress is on "in principle." There is no easy exit from ethical engagements, many of which are forced on us in much the same way that family relations are.

I assume that one can drift gradually and tactfully out of such relations without betraying anyone on the way out. The stress is on drift rather than on making an abrupt break. But if you are involved in thick relations, what you ought to do in order to maintain "healthy relations" in both senses is this: opt for relations that are good, and be good in those relations. What sort of lives can a-ethical men and women lead? Solitary perhaps, but there is no reason for them to be brutish and definitely not short.

So, ought we to remember ethically? My answer is

yes—if we are, and want to be, involved in thick relations. For the goodness within the relation, memory is crucial. It is crucial both as a constitutive part of our typical thick relations and as an affirmation of the relation. This is attested to by the expectation to be remembered after death. But it is not just for the goodness *within* the relation that memory is vital. It is also vital for the goodness *of* the relation. And I use the rather vague term *vital* advisedly, since memory, unlike shared history, is not a necessary condition of thick relations and yet it is tied up with caring— the ethical element that makes the relation good. So we ethically ought to remember on two counts: for the sake of the goodness *within* the relation and for the sake of the goodness *of* the relation.

4

EMOTIONS RECOLLECTED

Episodic Memory

P SYCHOLOGISTS call our memories of events
and dated objects *episodic memories*. These
are distinguished from memories of abstract objects such
as the multiplication table or the meaning of the word
multifarious—these memories are called semantic memories. In this chapter I want to deal with episodic memory
as the paradigm case for an ethics of memory. But another
kind of memory that is of great moment for an ethics of
memory is the memory of past emotions. Past emotions
can be about the objects of both semantic and episodic
memories. The philosopher Rudolf Carnap can remember his deep love for Esperanto, whereas the philosopher
Ludwig Wittgenstein may remember his utter disgust with
that artificial language. Both are memories of emotions

related to objects of semantic memory. But what I have in mind is memory of emotions tied to objects of episodic memory, such as my memory of a resentment I once felt about the way an official in passport control at Checkpoint Charlie treated me.

There is a great deal of literature on the emotions, and a great deal of literature on memory. There is little literature on remembering past emotions, and relatively little on hedonic psychology, in which remembering past experience plays an important role.[1] So part of what I shall try to do in this chapter is to give an account of what is involved in the memory of past emotions, informed by some findings from hedonic psychology.

Part of my account has to do with remembering past emotions and reliving these emotions in the present. Another part relates emotions and their memory to living in an enchanted world. I believe that the ethics of memory is a project that comes suspiciously close to viewing the world as enchanted. Memory as a project of gaining some form of immortality in a community of memory (see Chapter 1) can take the form of something akin to revivification. All this points to the reason why religion is so engaged with memory and can be regarded as the primary agency for treasuring memory. But "coming suspiciously close" to an enchanted world is a warning sign, not an inescapable trap. It does not say that the spell has been cast on all forms of memory that are relevant for the ethics of memory.

I would like to deal with the memory of emotions in general, and particularly with the memory of negative moral emotions, for which humiliation is a paradigm case. In Chapter 2, I declared my interest in remembering emotions as a way of knowing how the things we remember were felt at the time — a way of grasping the sense and the sensibility of past events needed for understanding and assessing the things we care about in the present, especially the people we care about. I use the term *emotion* both as a generic term that comes from feelings, sentiments, and affects but also as a contrastive term to moods. By *moral emotions* I mean emotions that motivate our ethical or moral conduct. The idea is that moral emotions motivate our moral behavior not just, and not even predominantly, through the way the emotions are experienced but through the way they are remembered. This holds true also for the way pleasure and pain affect our behavior. It is not so much the experience of pleasure and pain that makes us tick but rather the memory of pleasure and pain.

If this claim about our moral psychology is true, it should be pertinent to our ethics and politics. Here is an ethical and political question: Should we remember the hatred of our ancestors to their detractors, out of loyalty to our ancestors? The price of such memory can be high. It can poison our relationship with the innocent descendants of these oppressors.

Ought we to remember, ethically speaking, some of our own past emotions? It seems that a man may be rightly praised if (like the God of Jeremiah 2:2) he remembers and describes to his unfaithful wife the love she felt for him in her youth, when she wandered with him in the wilderness of a land that was not sown. By contrast, forgetting the love you once enjoyed can be taken as not being appreciative of the kindness you received. But before we address the question of which emotions we ought to remember, we face an antecedently nagging question, namely, What is it to remember an emotion and (even more nagging) what is it to forget an emotion? In remembering an emotion, do I remember my emotion toward others, their emotion toward me, or, possibly, other people's emotions toward each other? I shall here concentrate mainly on the first type of question—on my memory of my past emotions toward others.

Suppose I remember that I loved someone. I even remember when and where: say, in Paris in the springtime. Yet, I do not remember who she was. Does this mean that I remember my love, or rather that I forgot it? I shall come to these questions as I go along. I also want to add to this the vexing problem of love recollected as love revised.

The seventeenth-century French moralist Duc de la Rochefoucauld made the observation that there are very few people who are not ashamed of having been in love once they no longer are. And quite a few of them tend to revise the past. We may hear one say, "I wasn't really in love, it was more of an infatuation, a mere short crush," and so on.

A history of emotions tends to become revisionist history, a re-description of the emotions we had in the past. Revisionist history is not necessarily deluded history. For all we know we might have been deluded in the past. But then the question about remembering an emotion is, What are we supposed to remember: the emotion itself, or how we viewed the emotion in the past, or, if possible, both? Each of these possibilities has important implications, including moral implications, for how we assess our life, past and present.

I promised to dwell on negative moral emotions, and instead I find myself drumming up love. But then isn't love more fun than humiliation? Why dwell on negative emotions? There are two sets of reasons for the grim emphasis on negative emotions. One set has to do with what I dub *the priority of negative politics*, and the second set of reasons has to do with the centrality of wounding emotions that leave scars in the form of painful memories, in motivating our political actions.

Negative Politics

I opt to stress negative emotions—say, humiliation rather than pride, rejection rather than being recognized and accepted, feeling estranged rather than feeling at home—not as a matter of stylistic preference but as a strategy. The difference between dwelling on humiliation and not on recognition is not the same sort of difference as that between seeing the cup half empty and seeing it half full. The difference, I believe, cuts deeper. Is it not injustice rather than justice that "hurts us into politics"? And tyranny rather than freedom, poverty rather than equality, humiliation rather than dignity?

The situation is not unlike medicine as the art of curing and alleviating disease. It is disease that brings us to medicine, not health. This might strike us as a mere quibbling with words, and not as a genuine change in perspective. Curing a disease and maintaining health, you might say, are two sides of the same coin. Health and disease, like justice and injustice, are correlative terms that rise and fall as a pair, that are clarified and obfuscated together; dealing with the one is tantamount to dealing with the other. One cannot know what disease is without knowing what counts as health, and one cannot know what health is without knowing what counts as a disease. And the same must surely hold for justice and injustice.

I beg to differ. First, by deferring to theology. The shift from positive theology to negative theology was, I believe, a strategic move and not just a stylistic one. The idea was to shift the language of theology from attributing positive traits to God to expressing attributes that God does not have. The idea behind it was that nothing positive can be known about God, for He has nothing in common with other beings. No term that applied to Him retains its ordinary meaning, and thus His attributes should be glossed negatively. Theological assertions with regard to God, if true, indicate (more than state) what God is not. The gain from such an interpretative move is not new knowledge about God but rather the loss of the illusion of ever attaining such knowledge. We are incapable of knowing what God is—or even that He exists, since He does not exist in any of the ordinary senses in which things in the world exist.

What is so appealing about negative theology is the idea that on many occasions we recognize what is wrong with something without having a clear idea, or any idea at all, about what is right with it. In moral theory, as in constructivist mathematics, we should refrain from a facile use of the rule of the excluded middle, that is, the belief that just by negating what is wrong we will reach what is right. Right and wrong should be dealt with independently. Only after justifying independently what is right and what is wrong will the negation of the one yield the other.

While dealing independently with the right and the good and with the wrong and the evil, priority should be given to the negative side. Negative politics should take temporal priority in action, if not necessarily priority in preference, over positive politics, since eradicating cruelty and humiliation is more urgent than promoting and creating positive well-being. Thus, the politics of dignity should in my account be understood not as positive politics but rather as negative politics.[2] It should not address the question of how institutions can promote dignity in every human being by virtue of his or her being human, but rather it should ask how to stop humiliation. In the case of dignity, it seems that the negative turn in politics is almost a must. Dignity, unlike social honor, is not a positional good. It is supposed to be accorded to everybody, even to the one who is nobody, by virtue of the most universal common denominator of being human. Anybody should be recognized as a bearer of human dignity. Honor, in contrast, if it is bestowed on everybody, honors nobody. In the case of dignity, there is a concern that the mere treatment of human beings as humans has very little positive content. And the same goes for recognition, in the sense of accepting one as a human.

In many societies, at least in the old days, one could encounter a code of honor, usually an unwritten one. Such codes made it clear how to honor the other fittingly. But even in the case of honor—social honor—we recognize much better the negative cases, when one's honor is tarnished, than positive cases. While rewriting the last passage I was watching on television an NBA game between Indiana and Philadelphia. Mat Geiger, a gigantic basketball player, fouled badly the star of the Indiana team, Reggie Miller. Miller kept quiet, as we would expect him to do. But then Geiger knocked him brutally to the floor, a second flagrant foul. Our code of honor as sports fanatics is that Reggie should respond in kind. It is not good enough that the referee will take it upon himself to eject Geiger from the game. We all recognize Geiger's provocation as too much to bear. "We" includes Geiger's own coach: "I respect Reggie for what he did." Miller used his fists. It is not as if he was left unprotected and had to defend himself. He would have been defended by the referee and would not have had to bear the consequence of being ejected from the game himself. However, Miller's honor was violated, and we all recognized this as such.

The whole scene may strike us as a trifle childish, comic, and macho, but still, the code of *dis*honor is much clearer than the code of honor. In the case of dignity, there isn't even a code of dignity (unless we regard the charter of human rights as such a code). But we recognize dignity by the way we react to humiliation.

Jon Elster warns us against adopting goals that cannot

be realized through actions motivated only by the desire to realize them.[3] We can bring about those goals but not as an outcome of simple decision to bring them about. Our desire to forget can be such a case. Our desire to be spontaneous by trying hard to be spontaneous defeats the very goal we want to achieve, namely, spontaneity. This kind of self-defeating behavior has its counterparts in politics. Thus we may adopt political goals that cannot be achieved intelligently by willing them directly. It is not clear that a politics of dignity—of respecting human beings as human beings—does not fall under the category of essential by-products, in the language of Elster. That is, there is no way to bring about respect for human beings as human beings as a product of direct desire to respect others because we never encounter human beings just as human beings but as bus conductors or teachers. On the other hand, a decision not to humiliate and the goal of bringing about a non-humiliating society does not fall under the category of essential by-products.

If, as I suspect, the situations that negative politics addresses are more easily recognized, why does positive politics have such a hold on us? I believe that positive politics is backed by a metaphysical and religious picture of great moment. In the Pythagorean list of primary contrasts we find evil on the side of plurality, lack of boundaries, and darkness. On the side of the right and the just we find the one, the bounded, and light. The famous opening sentences of *Anna Karenina*, "Happy families are all alike. Every unhappy family is unhappy in its own way," is an expression of this Pythagorean picture. The good is one, the evil many. There is one way of being right and many ways of being wrong. All such clichés are expressions of that very same picture, a picture that is turned into a methodological principle; namely, there is no point in dealing with the many faces of injustice. Instead, it is much more economical to concentrate on the one positive idea of justice, and thereby gain coherent unity, rather than rely on scattered anecdotes about injustices. All this, I maintain, is a *picture*, not an argument, in favor of the positive approach. A formidable picture, but a picture nonetheless.

Adding Insult to Injury

The wise Earl of Chesterfield reported to his illegitimate son the observation that an injury is much sooner forgotten than an insult. Mental scars last longer than physical scars, and the effects of insults and humiliation last longer than mere physical pain. This is admittedly a rather vast and vague claim, but I hope that it is not an empty one and that it is worth clarifying. The hedge "mere physical pain" is important. It is meant to exclude one sort of unforgettable physical pain, that which is inflicted by torture. The scars due to torture are long-lasting.

The thoughtful and sorrowful philosopher Jean Amery,

who was captured and tortured by the Gestapo in 1943, is both an expert witness and a moral witness when it comes to torture. "If one speaks about torture one must [take] care not to exaggerate. What was inflicted on me in the unspeakable vault in Breendonk was by far not the worst form of torture. No red-hot needles were shoved under my fingernails, nor were any lit cigarettes extinguished on my bare chest . . . It was relatively harmless and it left no conspicuous scars on my body. And yet twenty two years later, on the basis of an experience that in no way probed the entire range of possibilities, I dare to assert that torture is the most horrible event a human being can retain within himself."[4]

Amery dismisses the idea that what is involved in torture is the loss of human dignity. "I must confess that I don't know exactly what that is: human dignity."[5] After all, there are those who might believe that in circumstances in which they cannot take their daily bath they lose their human dignity, he adds sarcastically. What Amery believes takes place right after the very first blow is a loss of "trust in the world." Different as the expressions "loss of trust in the world" and "loss of human dignity" strike us, Amery's gloss on loss of trust in the world comes very close to what I take to be humiliation, which is my rendering of "loss of human dignity." In Amery's account the tormentor causes the victim to realize that his physical and metaphysical being is not respected. By "metaphysical" I take him to mean that what the torturer, by his brutal act, denies is the victim's very human mode of existence.

In short, apart from inflicting horrific pain, torture in our culture constitutes an extreme form of humiliation that comes from one's being absolutely in the hands of the tormentor. By humiliation I mean treating humans as nonhumans. There are many forms of such treatment; torture is one of them. So torture is an extreme form of insult and injury, of pain and humiliation. The combination can be lethal, as it was in the case of Amery, who after many years took his own life.

It is silly, if not downright obscene, to regard torture as a mere "communicative act." Torture is, above all, excruciating pain, watched on many occasions with delight and hatred. But torture as experienced and torture as remembered can—and often do—diverge. In remembering torture, the victim dwells on the humiliation, whereas in experiencing torture he dwells on the pain.

Let me go back now to Chesterfield's comparison between the memory of insult and the memory of injury (that is, pain), leaving aside the confounding case of torture. Chesterfield's observation, properly understood, can make us see a lot. We do in fact remember the facts of physical pains to a remarkable degree, but we can hardly relive them. On the other hand, we can hardly remember insults without reliving them. Chesterfield's observation should therefore be qualified. It isn't necessarily the case that, in the *propositional* sense of remembering (remembering that so and so happened), we remember insults better than pains. In that sense we usually remember them both. But we remember insults better than pains in the sense of reliving them. The wounds of insult and humiliation keep bleeding long after the painful physical injuries have crusted over.

Reliving and Recollecting in Poetry

Poetry, good poetry, is torn between these two senses of remembering an emotion—remembering the emotion as expressed in a proposition, as opposed to the reliving the past emotion. William Wordsworth proposed a complicated third way between the cold contemplation of a past emotion and the hot reliving of it.[6] It is not true that poetry, for Wordsworth, is emotion recollected in tranquility. Rather, poetry for him is "the spontaneous overflow of powerful feelings." What Wordsworth advocates is first to contemplate our past emotion in tranquility, without reliving that emotion, and then "the tranquility gradually disappears and an emotion kindred to that which was before the subject of contemplation is gradually produced."[7]

Poetry, then, is not reliving a past emotion but rather

producing a new emotion similar to the past one. The emotions from the past that should nourish poetry are instinctive responses to what is beautiful and good in the rustic world of nature. Reliving emotions akin to the natural emotions of being at home in nature is an educated form of feelings "modified and directed by our thoughts."

The education of the powerful emotions that feed poetry should be conducted in the light of a radical principle ("elementary and grand"), the principle of pleasure. By pleasure Wordsworth means distilled biblical energy, and not mere polite pleasantness. The principle of pleasure is what constitutes, in Wordsworth's words, "the naked and native dignity of man." And thus, by implication, poetry expressing powerful recollected and transformed emotions guided by the pleasure principle is a manifestation of human dignity. Wordsworth believed that pleasure in the full sense of the word is what constitutes human dignity; pleasure is not—as the Christian idea has it—something base, if not beastly and degrading. Wordsworth's idea of pleasure as that which bestows and enhances human dignity is indeed a radical idea.

There is, however, a very different view on the relation between poetry and emotions. We can get the hang of it from an exchange between W. H. Auden and Stephen Spender, as reported by Spender. Spender once told Auden that he wondered whether he, Spender, ought to write prose instead of poetry.[8] Auden put his foot down. "You must write nothing but poetry, we do not want to lose you for poetry." "But do you really think I am good?" gulped Spender. "Of course," Auden stiffly replied. "But why?" asked Spender. "Because you are infinitely capable of being humiliated. Art is born of humiliation." By art Auden meant poetry. This is a vision of poetry as humiliation recollected in turmoil. Humiliation, unlike the rustic emotions of Wordsworth, if recollected, is relived.

By humiliation Auden had in mind, predominantly, sexual rejection mixed with frustrated love and hurt. But what does sexual defeat, painful as it may be, have to do with my strong sense of humiliation as rejection from the human commonwealth? Chester Kallman might have rejected Auden at a certain point as a sexual partner, but it never crossed his mind to reject him as a human being. Well, sexual rejection, even when it is not rejection of the other as a human being, is akin to humiliation insofar as it provides a good clue to what it is like to be humiliated in the strong sense. When your body is rejected, something very basic in you is rejected.

The comparison I am making between sexual humiliation and human degradation is not a moral one. Nobody has a right to impose himself or herself on another as a sexual partner, but everyone has the right not to be rejected by others as a human being. The comparison I am suggesting is a psychological comparison between these two kinds of humiliation. And one feature that the two types share is that you can hardly recollect the emotion without reliving it.

Fishing for Insults

Sexual humiliation—being rejected in body, not necessarily in soul, by a prospective or an actual partner—is no humiliation in my sense (unless the bodily rejection is propelled, say, by racist revulsion). Although it takes (at least) two for sexual relations, the defeated partner can declare, like Baudelaire: "I am the wound and the dagger."[9] Baudelaire did not necessarily believe that he is the Alpha and Omega in bringing about the wound. But he had an important part in bringing it on himself. This is not the case in my sense of humiliation. The wounded person is not a victim of his or her own doing.

Can we be both dagger and wound? Indeed we can. We do not just fish for compliments; we sometimes actively fish for insults as well. A curious phenomenon, but a phenomenon, I believe, nevertheless. Consider a the following practice (pointed out to me by Amos Tversky). After purchasing something, say shoes, people keep on with their shopping expedition and keep comparing the price of they shoes they just bought with the prices for similar shoes in other shop windows. These people are very likely to discover that they paid too much and that a true bargain lurked around the corner. This practice shows that although we may secretly hope that we bought well, we are often too experienced to really believe that. We do not always act simply to reduce dissonance but sometimes to enhance dissonance. In many cases of insults and social mortification, if we are not the knife's blade, we are at least its handle. Poetry, the "immortal wound" in the language of Robert Frost, is on occasion a documentation of a wound brought about by such a knife.

I am being slow in parting from poetry because I believe that good poetry is perhaps the best example of emotions recollected, in the sense of emotions relived. The task of unpacking the metaphors of emotional wounds and scars and of reliving the wound in nonmetaphorical terms is still ahead of us. But let me linger a bit longer on the metaphor of wound and scar.

Trauma

I mentioned already one argument for focusing on the memory of negative emotions in dealing with the memory of emotions in general. It was an additional argument to the one that highlights the role of negative emotions in negative politics. The argument hinges on the idea that negative emotions leave scars that are a strong analogue to memory traces. Scars, I maintain, like the master-metaphor trauma, which is just the Greek word for wound, are two formative metaphors that call for a gloss.

Trauma is a medical term that refers to a serious bodily injury or shock from an accident or external act of violence. When the term was adopted in psychoanalysis, it was designed to retain both connotations: of sudden, violent shock from an external source and of injury (in this case emotional injury) caused by the jolt. By *scar*, I understand the traces that the initial trauma leaves on the psyche, despite various degrees of healing. The language of trauma and scarring applies primarily to physical bodies. But these terms are so naturally, and perhaps universally, transferred to the psyche that the categorical distinction between the two is blurred.

Indeed, Freud sees in "archaic thinking" a system that pays no attention to the distinction between bodily symptoms and mental images, as both are in the business of transmitting similar information. He might render the ease with which we move from one sense of trauma and scarring to the other as a confirmation of the reality of archaic thinking rather than as a category mistake.

Freud in fact plays with two conflicting pictures: catharsis and trauma.[10] One is a wet picture, the other a dry one; the first is an image of purging the digestive system of an upsetting alien liquid element, the second of an injury and scar. In the image of catharsis, the pathogen is completely ejected, leaving no trace. In the image of trauma, the emotional discharge, the abreaction, still leaves a scar behind. The situation is like the two conflicting biblical pictures of forgiveness, which I develop in Chapter 6. One is a complete blotting out of the sin of the past—a kind of forgiveness of which only God is capable. The other is forgiveness as covering a stain. The stain is there, to be sure, but you do not act on it if you forgive.

Trauma, like a covered stain, still has effects. It makes the traumatized person react disproportionately to a present trigger on the strength of the injury from the past. Or it displaces that which brought the trauma about with a different object that is somehow associated with the object of the past. These are the two pathological manifestations of reliving the past.

Living and Reliving an Emotion

There is a style of philosophical analysis of emotions, not my style, that reminds me of the philosophical analysis of grammatical moods. Take the following three sentences:

    (a) The door is shut.
    (b) Shut the door!
    (c) Is the door shut?

All these sentences, so the analysis goes, have some content in common, to do with the door being shut. They differ, however, in their *moods*. That is, they differ in their attitudes toward the shared content. The indicative mood conventionally asserts its truth, the imperative mood orders it to be true, and the interrogative asks whether it is true. In the case of an emotion, as expressed by, say, "I am afraid of the enemy's shellfire," the analogical idea is to separate the descriptive content, namely, the enemy's shellfire, from my attitude to it, namely, that it is bad for me.

The combination of content and attitude, however, does not make this into an emotion statement. Something crucial is missing here, says a familiar analysis. The missing element is the feeling of the bodily changes that go with the reaction to the state of affairs described. In this style of analysis, the added element that turns the attitude toward the state of affairs into an emotion is a nonintentional feeling, sensation, or bodily change. Even if we render the added element as arousal or intensity, it is still nonintentional.

Thus, in this style of analysis, by reliving an emotion, say the reliving of my fear of the enemy's shellfire, I still hold it to be bad rather than exciting or exhilarating. But what makes it into reliving the old fear is that I regain now the old feelings of butterflies in my stomach or a dry mouth. The intensity may be different; my cold sweat now may not be as cold as it was then, but still. We may want to ask for even more. To relive the fear I have to conjure up some vivid images of the past shellfire, like jumping for cover or the shriek of the shell. We have to relive the past impressions by having vivid current ones, be it in our nightmares or in our daydreaming.

In saying that this is not my analysis, I do not wish for a moment to deny that in reliving a past emotion, all of the above may in fact take place—feelings, sensations, images, and all. What I do deny is that these are the constitutive elements both of the emotion itself and of reliving it. Living and reliving an emotion is a thoroughly intentional business, not a matter of a blind feeling's turning a cognitive state into an emotional one. What is essential to an emotion is the involved way in which the subject is engaged with the objects of his or her emotion.

Living an emotion is living an involved, not a detached, life. It is a way of seeing, reacting to, and thinking about the objects to which we relate in a certain way. The direction of fit between subject and objects of emotion can go in either direction—projecting the subject onto the objects, as in having a sentiment toward the objects, or being affected by objects, as in affects and passions. In one direction—from us to the object—we project our fears of the night onto a harmless bush, taking it to be a ferocious dog. In the other direction—from the object to us—we may encounter a lovely women and love her because of her loveliness. But in both directions we are involved. At the risk of circularity, I would say that emotions engage us with objects in a way that makes the objects lose their neutrality for us and become "marked": fearful, loveable, disgusting, exciting, and so on.

From my first-person perspective, if considerable time has passed since a certain event took place, I relive the emotion triggered by it if I find myself involved now with the objects of the past emotion in the way I was involved with them then. Reliving an emotion is being tied to an original event that is constitutive of the emotion (and not just a causal trigger of the emotion). In that sense, reliving an emotion is different from a manifestation of a disposition acquired in the past: with a disposition, the fact that there is no particular original event plays an essential role. In a disposition, the object that triggered the disposition, say, your first cigarette that launched you on a career of a chain smoker, can drop out of mind without your disposition to smoke changing in the least. On the other hand, your love for Jerusalem is affected if you forget Jerusalem.

Now, what is the difference between living an emotion for a long time, say living in humiliation, and reliving it? There is, I believe, no clear-cut distinction, as there are no clear-cut identity conditions for an emotion, through time. That is, there are no conditions that determine whether it is the same emotion all over again or a new emotion that was rekindled by the old objects from the past. The distinction between living in humiliation and reliving it is that in the case of reliving, a long period of time has passed since the original humiliation and the current involvement with the memory. For a long time one may manage not to brood on the painful memory. But then it comes back again and sometimes with a vengeance. Eichman's trial in Jerusalem forced many Nazi victims to relive the humiliations they suffered in the hell of the camps. My main claim is that it is hard to remember a past humiliation without reliving it.

By saying that it is hard yet not impossible to remember without reliving, I reveal that I am not making a conceptual claim but a psychological one. Be that as it may, the memory of humiliation is the bleeding scar of reliving it. Why is remembering humiliation a reliving of it? Humiliation, I believe, is not just another experience in our life, like, say, an embarrassment. It is a formative experience. It forms the way we view ourselves as humiliated persons — very much the way a serious failure in a project that matters to us greatly brings us to view ourselves as failures. Humiliation, in the strong sense, in being a fundamental assault on us as human beings, becomes constitutive of one sense of who we are. We may try to shrug it off and avoid living it on a daily basis. But if and when we remember it, and still recognize it as humiliation, then in the usual course of events we are more likely than not to relive it.

Reliving a Life

Hume presents us with an intriguing thought experiment. "Ask yourself, ask any of your acquaintances, whether they would live over again the last ten or twenty years of their life."[11] Hume is confident that their answer, as well as yours, will be a resounding no. Too many crucial details are missing in Hume's teaser. I shall try to provide some of them.

Suppose that what you are offered is to repeat the last ten years of your life exactly as they were, with no trace of memory from your previous experience of those ten years. Assume that the ten years that you are going to relive, if you accept the offer, are ten years added to your life and not a substitute for what awaits you. You will spend the rest of your life from the exact point you are in now, with the same state of mind and memories that you now have. Assume, further, that the last ten years in your life were not particularly bad, perhaps even reasonably good. There is of course a question as to what happens to the people involved in your life in the last ten years, how they are going to fare in the experiment. They should somehow agree to relive with you these last ten years, or the experiment won't work—if you really want to relive your life with the very same people and not with ersatz counterparts.

So let us assume, for the sake of our story, that they all agree to go along with your decision, and that they will relive with you the last ten years (including those who died in between). I'm not sure that the assumptions I added to Hume's experiment are his. He quotes Dryden, "and from the dredges of life, hope to receive what the first sprightly running could not give." I suspect that the point of the quotation is that what Hume had in mind was reliving the last ten years as a substitute for the next ten. For him, our opting to go on with our life stems from the illusionary hope that what is about to come will be better than what we had so far. This is, for Hume, the triumph of hope over experience.

If this is Hume's experiment, it is not mine. I offer a much better deal, an offer you cannot refuse: an extra ten years. Yet people presented with my version of the problem were split between those who opted for reliving the ten years and those who declined the offer. The question then is, Who should we agree with, those who accept the extra ten years or those who decline?

I would like to use Hume's thought experiment—on

my conditions—as a laboratory for testing two pictures of the way we lead, or should lead, our lives. I find both images partially true and partially misleading. Each should be corrected by using elements from the other. But first to the images, which, for lack of better titles, I shall call the *scientific picture* and the *literary picture* of life. In the scientific picture, life is presented along a homogenous axis of time, segmented into objective units of seconds, hours, days, and years. Along the time axis I can plot our hedonic course and compute the integral of how well I am. At each point in time there is an answer to the question how well I feel at the moment. And by summing up all such points I can answer the utilitarian's quintessential dream and answer his question, How happy was I in March?[12]

This picture may allow us to be even more ambitious and ask about the "state of the union," namely, How happy were Americans in April? It should enable us to see how Americans, as judged by a representative sample of them, felt in April.

Consider the following: while writing this passage I sip my coffee and thoroughly enjoy the experience. It is a trivial experience, nothing to write home about, and yet I feel good about it. There are many such moments each day. Why not repeat the experience of this very sipping, taking the chance Hume gave me to relive my last ten years?

Most of the experiences I had are unmemorable. They do not add up to a story, but they add up to making my last ten years rather good. The integral of my well-being in the last ten years suggests to me that I should repeat them. The curve of my well-being was plotted so that representative samples of points in my last ten years were taken mostly in moments in which I was not on guard. Still, it is the "scientific" record of my last ten years that tells me to go for it again. Although we tend to forget the trivial experiences that filled our lives in the last ten years (like the one with the coffee), they are the ones that truly make up our lives.

In the conflicting literary picture of life we are the authors of our lives, and we had better make sure that they add up to something meaningful. If you are (to misquote T. S. Eliot) going to measure your life with coffee spoons, then you are doomed to a meaningless life. Meaningful life is the life of reflective memory, not the life of blind experiences; it is life that can be told in a good *Bildungs-roman*. In this image, reliving the last ten years of my life with no additional reflections is like having to read the same chapter in a novel twice because of a printer's mistake: no development, no contribution to my self-understanding, no nothing. More and more coffee sips—this is all that will be left to do. Now what does all of this have to do with remembering emotions? A great deal.

Moods and Emotions

Emotions, I submit, go well with the literary picture of life, whereas moods (nongrammatical moods) go well with the scientific picture. We remember emotions just as we remember storms, but we find it very hard to remember moods just as we find it hard to remember the weather conditions in ordinary days. Emotions go well with a plot, but moods can hardly go with a story. Remember E. M. Forster's distinction: "The king died and then the queen died" is a story; "The king died and then the queen died of grief" is a plot. Plots add causal relations and motivations. Moods are temporary frames of mind; being sulky or being cheerful are such frames. If they recur habitually, they may also be character traits. But I have in mind here moods as temporary frames of mind. So in saying that Lenora is gloomy, I refer to her temporary mood and not to her as a gloomy person. She may be gloomy now but in general be quite cheerful. Moods are hardly registered. It takes Proust to record moods, but it takes no more than Somerset Maugham to weave emotions, such as anxiety about one's means of livelihood, into a plot.

What makes moods hard to remember is that, unlike emotions, they lack a specific intentional object. They may have objects as their cause, indeed sometimes trivial ones. You get back the coin you inserted in the telephone box after completing your call, and it brightens up your day. But your mood is not about the coin.

You do not believe that the black cat that crossed your way is going to bring you real harm. But the black cat brought bad thoughts and uneasy associations, and your mood has been changed for the worse. Still, your mood is not about the black cat.

So moods are no little emotions, even if trivial causes can bring about changes in our moods. Moods are very important in our life—the life we lead, not the life we remember. Moods affect our memory. Good moods promote good positive memories; bad moods promote strong negative memories. But what we are interested in is not the mood affecting memory but the memory of moods.

The differences between life remembered and life experienced comes into sharp focus in a set of revealing experiments conducted by Daniel Kahneman and others. Subjects were told to put their hands in cold water. In one trial the subjects kept their hands at 14 degrees centigrade for sixty seconds and then removed them altogether. The second trial lasted thirty seconds longer; at first the subjects (the same subjects who had participated in the first trial) kept their hands in the unpleasantly cold water (14 degrees) for sixty seconds, as before, but for the remaining thirty seconds the experimenter raised the temperature a bit (to 15 degrees, which feels noticeably more lukewarm). After an intermission of seven minutes the same subjects were called back for a third experiment. This time, they were given the opportunity to choose between repeating the first trial (known to us to be shorter) and the second one (known to us to be longer).

Most of the subjects preferred to repeat the experiment which lasts longer. We know that this second experiment contains all the pain of the first experiment, plus an extra 30-seconds'-worth of a somewhat lesser pain. Kahneman's explanation of this strange preference is that memory of a painful experience is determined not by the duration of the experience but by its peak point and its end point. Indeed, it is remembered by the difference between the painful sensations at these two points. Imagine that the subjects ranked the painful sensation of a hand in 14-degree water as 9 on a scale of 0 to 10, as compared to a ranking of 4 for the sensation when the temperature of the water was raised to 15 degrees. Then, the difference $(9 - 4)$ in the second trial is lower than in the second trial $(9 - 0)$, regardless of how long the experiment lasted.

Peak points and end points go well with the idea of a story that is being remembered; not so the actual duration. We value greatly a happy ending. And we value very differently a life that started badly and ended happily as compared with a life that went in the other direction, even if the integrals of the experienced well-being in the two courses of life are the same.

Are we wrong to judge our life by the way we remember

it rather than by the way we experience it? The so-called scientific picture says yes; the literary picture says no. And I say (timidly perhaps) that the truth is in a combination of the two—a picture, that is, that can combine our experienced life, which is colored by moods, with our remembered life, which contains emotions. There is, however, one other picture that I would like to mention, which challenges an assumption taken for granted both by the scientific and the literary images. The common assumption is that life should be measured by *addition*, not by *subtraction*, and that the difference between the two pictures is in what it is that should be added. The scientific picture contends that the addition should encompass all the experiences in one's life, remembered as well as unremembered. The literary picture, in contrast, contends that the addition should comprise all the highlights that are remembered and that go into a coherent story of one's life.

But there is a picture of life which views it on a subtraction, not an addition, model, and this picture has been very influential historically. The idea is that one shapes one's life as a sculptor shapes his statue in marble: by removing the inessential parts so as to "bring to life" the figure that preexisted in the marble. Emotions, on this model, are what should be sculpted away, as an inessential part of one's life that stands in the way of revealing the true statue that is in the marble. Stoicism, epicureanism, monasticism, and Buddhism all share, in one way or another, the sculpting model of life. A perfect statue, that is, a perfect life that the self-sculpting artist shapes, is a life of *apatheia*, of negating one's emotions and of adopting a noninvolved posture toward life.

I mention this picture, but I shall not probe it. Not because I have no argument against it but because it is not an option of life for me or for anyone I know. I consider not being an option as being, in a way, enough of an argument.

A Revisionist History of Emotions

I mentioned already two senses of remembering an emotion—a cold memory couched only in propositions ("remembering that") and a hot memory of reliving. My mother died a long time ago. I remember what I felt for her at the time, and I know what I feel for her now. But I also remember how painful it was when I gradually discovered that I am hardly able to conjure up her image in my mind's eye. I remember—propositionally—a great deal of how she looked, but I don't retain anymore a vivid image of her. I feel bad about it, as if my loyalty to her is in question, as if the kind of memory I retain is not good enough. I do not think that a visual image is either necessary or sufficient for remembering my mother. But then, why do I feel bad for not having a vivid visual memory of her?

We tie visual images with the reliving of emotions and the lack of an image as the waning of an emotion. A visual image gives us a sense of reliving an emotion in the imagination. But imagination means two things: the ability to conjure images, and thereby to consider things that are not present but that exist or existed; and the ability to fantasize unreal things. Memory is constrained by the reality of the past. Imagination, in the fanciful sense of the word, is not. Revision of our past history asks us to look for that which is absent but not to invent that which did not exist. But then revisionist history of emotions is a complicated matter indeed, since a great deal of what takes place in redescribing our past emotions is reevaluating them, sometimes in light of what became clear later. Our inability to relive an emotion is one of the things that make us reevaluate or revise our account of our past emotion. If I fail to remember vividly someone I hated in the past, I might find it hard to believe that I ever hated him. I might just as well reevaluate my emotion by downgrading its intensity. I sort of disliked him, but I didn't really hate him.

Reevaluating emotions can take the Nietzschean form of valuing an emotion differently from the way we used to value it in the past. Thus, pity may turn from a positive into a negative emotion and become sentimentality.

Think of all the films you adored in the past but that you find pretty embarrassing today. I believe that a great deal of your change of heart has to do with sentiments expressed in those films; you reevaluate them and what may have struck you at the time as simple and pure in those emotions strikes you now as unbearably naive.

To wit, the evaluation that goes with an emotion is part of the identity conditions of the emotion. When you evaluate an emotion differently, it is not the same emotion that you just consider in a new light but a different emotion altogether. I hold this extreme view weakly, for I am not sure about the whole idea of having identity conditions for emotions.

A Cross between Care and Caring

In the traditional picture, we humans encounter the world on a neutral basis. Each one of us is endowed with cognitive and perceptual abilities that enable us to form a personal theory about the indifferent objects that surround us in the world. Then and only then, we exchange views with others in the market of ideas and calibrate our views with those of others.

Heidegger in *Being and Time* promotes a different picture. It comes from his analysis of our human mode of existence. There are preconditions for human understanding that saturate our everyday existence. In his account, you do not approach things in the world as indifferent objects detected by your sense perception. Your primary encounter with the world is practical. What matters to you in each encounter is that you will be able to figure out how to use the things that are ready at hand. Their function in your life, rather than their perceptual properties, is what matters to you most. The world is a huge workshop in which each of us tries to find a place, a proper function, and an apt use for our tools. We are involved with the world as workers, not as impartial spectators.

True, there are objects in our world that we merely contemplate, that are present to us without our being involved instrumentally with them. An example would be when the stars in the sky are not involved in navigation. But these objects play a secondary role in the way we approach our world, according to Heidegger. So the primary objects are judged instrumentally; the secondary detected objects are viewed contemplatively.

But then there is a third category of entities whose mode of being is like ours, namely, our fellow human beings. Our encounter with *them* is different from our encounter with the first two categories. Heidegger's recognition that everyday ontology should distinguish between objects with which we are involved and those just present to us, I maintain, should be paralleled by a distinction with regard to human beings. There are those with whom we are involved—that is, with whom we have thick relations—and others of whom we have only a thin idea of their existence. Being involved does not mean being positively involved. We are very much involved with people we hate. But this distinction between the two types of humans is part of our fundamental ontology, the ontology that analyzes our human mode of being. There are, I believe, deep moral consequences for this division that can be encapsulated into an Auden-like paragraph: Let us honor if we can the hypothetical man, though we know none but the involved one.

The interest in the way we remember our past emotions is an interest, among other things, in the relation between ethics and morality. Ethics is based on thick and involved relations in which emotions toward the other play a major role. Morality walks on a thin rope, with very little emotion among mere human beings to keep the rope tight. As Adam Smith expressed it, the proper emotions to make morality go round are the emotions that a detached and yet sympathetic observer would have. Priority should not be given to our involved relations. In Adam Smith's account I should not grieve my mother's death more than a detached observer would have or should have.

In my account, an emotional relation to someone or to something is an involved emotional relation.[13] Being in-

THE ETHICS OF MEMORY

terested emotionally in other people is being involved
with them for better or for worse. For better if the domi-
nant emotion is of love and caring, for worse if it is of hate
and spite. Emotions not only color but also constitute our
most important relations to others. We expect parental
love not just to color the relation between parents and
children but to be a constitutive part of those relations —
the mere biological parenthood of, say, a male sperm do-
nor is not enough to constitute what we regard as parental
relations.

A social reality saturated with positive emotional bonds
is the cement of an ethical community. But an important
part of what holds an ethical community based on thick
relations together is the memory of past emotions, of great
solidarity in trying times and perhaps enmity toward a
common enemy.

Disengagement, estrangement, and alienation — the
solvents of the ethical community — loosen the memory of
shared emotions. Solidarity wavers when the memory of a
strong feeling of solidarity fades away.

Living in an emotionally involved world is living a risky
life. The risks are on the whole worth taking, but they are
risks nevertheless. An ethical community makes an effort
to channel the hazardous emotions of an involved society
into emotions of care and caring. But then what are the
risks of an emotionally involved individual and an emotionally involved society?

Undisciplined Squads of Emotions

Jean-Paul Sartre held a curious theory of emotions, or rather a sketch of such a theory.[14] Living in the world in constant states of uncertainty creates in us a tendency for magical thinking, as a substitute for causal thinking. Emotions are a species of magical thinking, due to our inability to have a sure sense of what is going to happen to us in the world, and with this a lack of control over our life. Thus, faced with the uncertainty of possessing the grapes, we magically turn them into sour grapes, so as not to have wanted them. There is one element in Sartre's account that I find very valuable — it is the idea that emotions, like magic, make us dwell in an enchanted world, in Weber's sense of the term. We live in an animated world fraught with objects that have their own intentions, for ill or good. Thus animated and personified, this world is a charmed place, but we are bound to get its casual network of relations wrong. And it is exactly this fact, of getting the casual relations wrong, that is the price we pay for living in an emotionally charged world. In this view, it is our emotions that cast the spell on a haphazard world.

In science — in good science, that is — the practitioners are emotionally detached. Not of course detached from their work — they may feel passionately about it — but toward the objects of their research. The vision of science as a detached activity is not grossly off the mark. The success of science is due to our ability to work in a disenchanted world in which casual relations are more apparent than in an enchanted world. So we want love and we want rationality, but we should be clear about what we get from the one and what we get from the other. In an ethical community it is love, or rather caring, that should reign supreme; in a merely moral community, mere rationality will do.

5

A MORAL WITNESS

Marks of a Moral Witness

C OLLECTIVE MEMORY has agents and agencies entrusted with preserving and diffusing it. One sort of agent should be of particular concern for those who are interested in the questions of what we should remember and what, if anything, we should forget—that is, for those who are interested in the ethics of memory. The agent I have in mind is the moral witness. In this chapter I shall try to give an account of the moral witness, leaving aside the distinction between morality and ethics, to which I shall return at the end. My account is partly an explication and partly a stipulation of the meaning of the expression *moral witness*, but it is mainly a phenomenological description of being a moral witness.

To her famous "Requiem" with its prominent line, "I

stand as a witness to the common lot, survivor of that time and place," Anna Akhmatova prefaced what she called "Instead of a Preface." In it she writes: "In the terrible year of the Yezhov terror, I spent seventeen months waiting in line outside the prison in Leningrad. One day somebody in the crowd identified me. Standing behind me was a woman with lips blue from the cold, who had of course never heard me called by name before. Now she started out of the torpor common to us all and asked me in a whisper (everyone whispered there) 'Can you describe this?' and I said 'I can.' Then something like a smile passed fleeting over what had once been her face."[1]

I believe that this passage provides the key to some important features of the moral witness, or the would-be moral witness. First, what should a witness witness in order to be regarded as a moral witness? He or she should witness—indeed, they should experience—suffering inflicted by an unmitigated evil regime. Yezhovschina, the Stalinist reign of terror through the secret police as directed by Nikolai Ivanovich Yezhov (1937–38), is a paradigm case of an unmitigated evil force inflicting immeasurable pain. Thus, to become a moral witness one has to witness the combination of evil and the suffering it produces: witnessing only evil or only suffering is not enough.

Surviving a natural disaster against all odds and vividly telling the story of the destruction and suffering that it has caused does not turn the survivor into a moral witness. To view a natural disaster as morally neutral is of course to view it from a disenchanted point of view. In a religious worldview a flood, say, may be regarded as a punishment for moral depravity. In such a world Noah, the survivor of the destructive biblical flood, can be a moral witness.

If, within a disenchanted worldview, a natural disaster is experienced as human suffering without the presence of an evil force, what about evil without suffering? Suppose that an evil agent has a wicked plan and suppose, further, that a courageous witness leaks the secret plan with the hope of preempting it: Is this witness a moral witness? In my account, it may well be the case that the leaking witness is a witness and that he is moral; yet he is not a "moral witness."

Being a moral witness involves witnessing actual suffering, not just intended suffering. A moral witness has knowledge-by-acquaintance of suffering. But does acquaintance mean experiencing the suffering first-hand—as a victim—or can one know it as a sympathetic bystander, observing the suffering without being a victim oneself? Consider the nun in Istanbul who, from her window, watched the massacre of the Armenians, and then with great personal risk took it upon herself to report what she saw to the world: Is she eligible for being considered a moral witness?

I think that observers who are not themselves the suffering victims of evil can serve as moral witnesses, but such observers are not our central, uncontroversial, standard cases. The paradigmatic case of a moral witness is one who experiences the suffering—one who is not just an observer but also a sufferer.

The moral witness should himself be at personal risk, whether he is a sufferer or just an observer of the suffering that comes from evil-doing. An utterly sheltered witness is no moral witness. There are two senses of risk here. There is the risk of belonging to the category of people toward whom the evil deeds are directed, and there is the risk of trying to document and record what happens for some future use. We may thus speak of the risk of being a victim and the risk of being a witness. Witness-risk can be a vicarious victim-risk that comes from witnessing the suffering of people who are near and dear to you. Indeed, many potential witnesses are blackmailed into silence not by direct threats to themselves personally but by threats directed to their relatives and friends. Be that as it may, a moral witness is at risk.

But then do foreign journalists whose professional business is to report the evil deeds of evil regimes, and who sometimes take tremendous risks while doing so, count as moral witnesses? The question is not whether hard-boiled "war correspondents" want the title of moral witness added to their name. They may find it an insulting title, as

if implying that they are going soft and becoming senti-
mental moralists. The question is for us, not for them. Do
we want to ascribe to professional journalists the title of
moral witnesses? The title should go to one whose testimonial mission has a moral purpose. Just reporting on evil
because it is interesting and makes a good story, even if
the reporting is risky, is to report with no moral purpose.

As a war correspondent on the side of the Nazis, the
Austro-Italian writer Curizo Maleparte was present at the
very heart of darkness.[2] We can assume that he took some
risk in keeping the diary that he kept, and his account of
evil and suffering in *Kaputt* is astonishingly vivid and powerful. Yet he strikes us as someone who is more amused
than disturbed. The atrocities he encounters as an observer are for him good stories. He is not immoral but
amoral. He is not one of the sadistic Nazis who took pictures as mementos of great fun. But still his amorality
disqualifies him to be a moral witness. In short, a moral
purpose is an essential ingredient of a moral witness.

Hope against Hope

Should a moral witness be guided by hope? Should his or
her testimony be an expression of hope? If so, hope for
what, and hope for whom? Was the fleeting smile on
"what had once been the face" of that tormented woman

standing behind Akhmatova an expression of hope—the hope of discovering an able moral witness who will describe her plight?

Hope, along with the theological virtues of love, faith, and charity, is a religiously charged notion. Hope is the eschatological expectation of future salvation. In the Christian New Testament, God himself is described as the "God of hope" (Romans 15:13). This is an important reminder, since the idea of the moral witness itself is under the suspicion of being a disguised secular version of the religious witness, the martyr, the *sahid* (the Greek and Arabic terms both meaning originally "witness"). The religious witness, through his suffering and ultimate sacrifice, expresses in times of trial his confidence in a world that against all appearances is still governed by a moral authority and a supreme and just judge, that is, by God. The hope is that at the end of days an everlasting perfect moral universe will be installed on earth. There are many pseudo-secular versions of this vision of historical messianic time, in which three unities will prevail: the unity of man with himself, the unity of man with his fellow men, and the unity of man with nature. Hope, then, is hope about a harmonious moral (ethical) order toward which history is striving in spite of temporary setbacks.

Is the idea of the moral witness a disguised form of religious hope in trying days? Is the moral witness a forward-looking creature even when his testimony is about the past? Akhmatova herself was mesmerized by the image of Lot's wife—the ultimate backward-looking creature who knew very well that she was being rescued from the destruction of Sodom and yet could not help looking back at what was once her past and her home.

I stress the eschatological sense of hope in questioning the relation between being a moral witness and the expression of hope, since this takes us to the intriguing thesis that morality (ethics) does not stand on its own but is grounded in religion. One has to distinguish between two senses in which morality is allegedly grounded in religion: the genetic (historical) sense, and the justificatory sense. The genetic sense is very much Max Weber's idea of morality as historically emerging from religion. But one may find G. E. M. Anscombe making a stronger claim, to the effect that a great deal of modern moral theory makes sense and can be justified only in a religious frame based on the idea of a divine lawgiver. The way I understand Miss Anscombe's claim is that the only justification for morality can be found in religion, and that it has no autonomous status of its own.[3]

Indeed, one may trace the same ambiguity in the kindred claim of political theology to which both Michael Bakunin and Carl Schmidt subscribe. Their claim is that politics is strongly grounded in an explicit or tacit theol-

ogy. Bakunin, I believe, understands this claim as a justificatory one, namely, that the only justification for the
state is in theological terms, and since this in principle
cannot be more than an illusionary justification, theology
and the state should both be brought down together.[4]
Schmidt I understand as making the genetic claim, that
there are very strong structural similarities between religion and the secularized theory of the state that emerged
from religion, but I do not see him making the justificatory claim.[5]

My view is that both relations, between religion and
morality and between religion and politics, are genetic relations that are based on strong structural analogies. Yet
the underpinnings of morality and ethics can, and hence
should, be based on autonomous justification. For one
thing, such justification demands less from us by way of
believing.

The moral witness, in my account, is not a poor substitute for the religious witness of hope. The idea of the
moral witness has content of its own. At the same time I
do not wish to deny the possibility that the idea of a moral
witness is a historical heir to the idea of the religious martyr as a witness. Note, however, that it is an heir with a
twist: the martyr witnesses and then dies, whereas the
moral witness has to live in order to serve. Still, I do deny
that the notion of the moral witness has no justification in

humanistic terms. More specifically, I deny that the sense of hope involved with the notion of the moral witness is akin to the eschatological hope for salvation in a messianic era.

The hope with which I credit moral witnesses is a rather sober hope: that in another place or another time there exists, or will exist, a moral community that will listen to their testimony. What is so heroic in this hope is the fact that people who are subjected to evil regimes intent on destroying the fabric of their moral community easily come to see the regime as invincible and indestructible and stop believing in the very possibility of a moral community. Being a helpless inmate in a Nazi concentration camp or a Bolshevik gulag can make you believe that the thousand years Reich or the unstoppable juggernaut of communist triumph is just the way of the world. The disparity of power between victim and perpetrator confirms every minute what seems to be the invincibility of the regime. Under such adverse conditions, to believe in what would under normal circumstances be a rather reasonable belief—namely, that the evil power is limited and temporary—is hard indeed. The belief, under such conditions, in the possibility of a moral community calls for a veritable leap of faith. But then the moral witness does not have to have the assured confidence of a sleepwalker that is manifested by a religious witness.

Abraham, the great believer, was praised as the one "who against hope believed in hope" (Romans 4:18). Given Sarah's old age, Abraham still hoped that what was promised to him, to be a father of many nations, would nevertheless become true. The moral witness, on my account, does not have to hope against hope.

Hope against Hope is the English title of Nadezhda Mandelstam's great moral testimony on the Yezhovschina. This was not the title she gave to her manuscript, but it was a favorite expression of hers, and the translator deemed it a fitting title for her book. But Nadezhda— whose name means hope in Russian—has herself given the title *Hope Abandoned* to her second volume, which is as much a moral testimony as *Hope against Hope*.[6]

Moral witnesses can—and often do—act like survivors of a shipwreck who find themselves on a desert island and figure that they have nothing to lose and perhaps something to gain by sending a bottle with a message into the ocean. (Anthony Kenney thinks that the same idea holds even for prayers to God.) There is nothing irrational in sending the written message with little expectation but with great hope that it will reach helpful eyes. This, I maintain, is the kind of hope the moral witness can assume. There is, however, one important difference between one who sends a bottle with a message and a moral witness. The sender of the bottle does not take any risk, since there is nothing to lose in his case and only something to gain, though the probability is miniscule. To be a moral witness, on the other hand, is all about taking risks.

What about the state of mind of someone who is committed to documenting on a daily basis the evil he encounters with absolutely no hope that his account will ever be read by a moral community? Perhaps Victor Klemperer wrote his compelling diaries in that state of mind.[7] Indeed, I believe that Adam Czerniakow, the leader of the Judenrat in the Warsaw Ghetto, wrote his diary—arguably the most compelling diary of that dark era—in such a state of mind.[8] But Czerniakow's suicide colors the case I am going to make, so I shall stick with Klemperer.

Perhaps Klemperer wrote out of his own need to settle scores with the evil he met but with no hope for an outside moral gaze. Yet there was, I believe, a moral purpose in Klemperer's documentation of his daily life. It can be stated in the language of the Mishnaic saying: "Where there is no human being, be one." One might say, then, that Klemperer wrote his diary to his own future self, a self that could turn out to be the sole surviving decent human being.[9] Klemperer is definitely a witness, and a moral one. But is he a moral witness?

One can wonder if it is psychologically possible to write a truly private diary, which is never intended to be read by anyone other than yourself. Of course we can easily imagine a shady art dealer, like Lord Duveen, who keeps a notebook documenting his "authenticated" pictures very much for himself. But this is not the kind of private diary I have in mind. The universal hope of anyone writing a diary is that it will be read—perhaps posthumously—by a sympathetic reader. My claim is that *psychologically* every writer of a private diary has a secret wish, not necessarily an unconscious wish, that the diary would one day be read by another person.

Wittgenstein famously renders the project of writing a strictly private diary, in the sense of a diary whose author is the only one who can in principle understand it, as a conceptual impossibility. Not being able to conduct a private diary in Wittgenstein's strong sense of private does not mean that one is unable to compose a diary for one's own exclusive consumption in the years to come. Being the sole user of a public library does not preclude others from using the library in principle, but still, as a matter of fact, the library may have one user only.

Practical privacy is both a conceptual and a psychological possibility. It may very well be the case that Klemperer wrote his diary with practical privacy in mind, and yet he obviously hoped for a moral bond between the Klemperer who was writing between 1933 and 1945 and the future Klemperer, if there was going to be one. The minimal moral community, in my account, is between oneself and the one's future self, who the current self hopes will retain a moral outlook. The minimal hope of a moral witness is, I believe, a belief about the future self. Perhaps this belief is too thin to do much work, but it is the minimal ethical community I can think of.

The Moral Ambiguity of the Moral Witness

Let me throw out a very curious question: Can a traitor aspire to be a moral witness? The point of the question is to explore how immoral one can be while aspiring to be a moral witness. The case of Josephus Flavius highlights this point. Josephus is without question the most important witness to the turbulent years leading to the first-century revolt of the Jews against the Romans, including to the revolt itself. He is also the only source for his own treacherous behavior.

Josephus was born to a priestly Jewish family in Jerusalem. At the outbreak of the Jewish war in 66 C.E., he was assigned by the Council of Sages in Jerusalem to be in charge of the northern front in the Galilee. The crucial battle against the Romans took place around the city of Jotapata. When the city fell, Josephus escaped through a cistern into a hidden cave in which forty other fighters also took refuge. Their hiding place was discovered and

Josephus, whose life had been assured to him through a deal with the Romans, tried first to persuade his comrades to surrender to the Romans. When he failed, he behaved as if he was willing to join his fellow Jews in a scheme to commit communal suicide.

He artfully arranged to cast the lots in such a way that he and one other man would be the last ones left to kill themselves. At that point he persuaded this fellow soldier to surrender to the Romans. Once on the side of the Romans, he joined them in the siege of Jerusalem and tried to help them, with no success, to persuade the rebels in the city to lay down their arms so as to save the city from destruction. But the Jews in Jerusalem regarded him as a despicable traitor and even managed in one case to injure him.

Josephus viewed himself as a man with a mission. While in the cave, he believed that "it would be a betrayal of the commands of God if he died before imparting his message."[10] He took his mission to be not unlike that of the prophet Jeremiah at the time of the first temple, which was to tell the Jews that there is life for the Jewish people even after the destruction of their temple. The Zealot Elazar ben Yair, in contrast, did go through with a mutual suicide pact with his people at the fortress of Masada because he lost hope in the possibility of having a future for the Jewish people.

Let us assume that the sense of mission to provide a full and accurate written account of the war of the Jews against the Romans is what motivated Josephus or served as his reason to betray the people in the cave while remaining loyal to the Jewish people in his own eyes. Given this charitable assumption, we may proceed to ask whether Josephus can be considered a candidate for being a moral witness.

Before we even reach the question of "useful treason," we must disqualify the historical Josephus as a moral witness. The change he underwent from being Josephus ben Mattias into Flavius Josephus, a client of the emperor Flavius, means that he wrote his formidable testimony with the aim of exculpating the cruel Romans and shifting the moral blame for the destruction of the temple onto one particular segment of the Jewish people—the Zealots. Still, while not meeting one criterion for being a moral witness, namely, exposing an evil force, Josephus excelled in meeting the other criterion, that of describing the suffering of the victims from the perspective of an eyewitness. This is why the case of the historical Josephus is confusing.

I have already floated the idea that one can be moral and a witness and still not be a moral witness. *Moral witness* is a case of an unbreakable expression in the way *wet nurse* is: one can be a nurse and be wet from the rain but still not be a wet nurse in the required sense. The issue I am trying to raise with the case of Josephus is the converse, the possibility of not being moral and yet being a moral witness. We should remind ourselves that being a moral witness means being subject to an extremely harsh reality. In such a reality it is possible that one's chances of survival are slim and that the only way of enhancing the chance to stay alive and be able to tell one's story is by betraying, in one way or another, one's fellow victims.

A paradigmatic case of a moral witness should be someone whose morality is not in question. But a moral witness may still be one who compromises his morality for the sake of surviving, especially if the aim is to survive as a witness. I do not feel at ease with this stand, but it is a necessary stand given the horrendous circumstances in which some people may find themselves in the struggle to survive—circumstances for which we need a moral witness in the first place.

Truth and Authenticity

Pimen, the old monk in Aleksandr Pushkin's play *Boris Godunov*—a play that was turned by Mussorgsky into a famous opera—is an honest-to-God chronicler.[11] Indeed, he finds the role of writing the historical events of Russia, without explanations and interpretations, a sacred task that should be carried out selflessly and anonymously. He knows all too well the extent and the meaning of Boris's crime, which brought about the assassination of the legitimate heir to the czar. Pimen piously hopes that heavens will settle the score for the crime, whereas he himself has to stick to what truly occurred—factually, objectively, and in the right order. The role of the royal chronicler is to record the right succession. But the succession to Ivan is in crisis, so much so that Boris's crime is overshadowed by the pretender Gregory, who was destined to become a chronicler and in an act of hubris aspired to be the czar, thus shaking the very idea of legitimacy.

It would be very wrong to say that the perspective of the chronicler is legality, while that of the moral witness is morality. In Pimen's chain of being the hubris of Gregory and the crime of Boris are terrible sins. But it is for heaven to judge and for him to record. To be a truthful chronicler is to be a perfect historical seismograph, to record accurately the vibrations of history. But a seismograph does not tell us what it is like to be in an earthquake. For that we need a moral witness.

A moral witness is a species of an eyewitness. An eyewitness should tell us what his or her eyes saw, and not provide testimony based on hearsay. The canon of judging the truthfulness of a moral witness should be the canon of judging the reliability of an eyewitness. The adjective *moral* has to do with the content of the testimony, not with the epistemological status of what the moral witness witnessed. Yet it would be extremely odd to cross-examine Akhmatova's poems in court, or to put Primo Levi under oath. Not because it is beneath their dignity to be questioned but because it is pointless. But is it?

The Hebrew and Yiddish writer K. Zetnik (a telling pseudonym of Jehiel Dinur) was one of the very few natives of Zaglembia (Poland) to have survived the war. There was perhaps no one else with Zetnik's sense of burning mission to be a moral witness, who desperately wanted to survive for the sole purpose of telling his horror story of the Holocaust. He became recognized at the time, through his books, as an authoritative moral witness and as such he was invited to testify at the Eichmann trial in 1961.

He collapsed on the witness stand, but his testimony stands, and it is: "This is actually the history of the Auschwitz planet, the chronicles of Auschwitz. I myself was at Auschwitz camp for two years. The time there is not a concept as it is here in our planet. Every fraction of a second passed there was at a different note of time. And the inhabitants of that planet had no names. They breathed and lived according to different laws of Nature. They did not live according to the laws of this world of ours and they did not die."[12]

What he tried to convey by these words is the idea that because Auschwitz was "another planet," there are no adequate terms, at least none that are acceptable in court, to convey what he experienced there. His answer to the question addressed to Akhmatova, Can you describe this? is, in a way, no. But then, what is the "this" that a moral witness is supposed to describe truthfully?

Uncovering the Evil

The moral witness plays a special role in uncovering the evil he or she encounters. Evil regimes try hard to cover up the enormity of their crimes, and the moral witness tries to expose it.

As it became clear to the SS command that Germany was going to lose the war, it launched an operation that could be dubbed by us operation Black Hole. Its aim was to make sure that no ray of truth escaped about what took place in the death camps. No witness was to survive, no document was to remain, and all traces of the "ovens" were to be eradicated so that no material sign would remain to attest to the evil.

No matter what assurances the SS officers received from Heinrich Himmler that what they were doing was "the decent" thing to do, they knew very well that they were engaged in what would be a colossal crime in the eyes of the world. This explains their hasty effort to get rid of potential witnesses, through so-called death marches away from the advancing liberating armies. But then the extent of the Nazi crime was so enormous, and involved so many people in so many places, that it was quite irrational of the perpetrators to expect that they would succeed in getting away with it by some kind of "black hole" operation. By the same token, the victims too were terrified at the prospect that the attempted cover-up—rational or not—might succeed. So perpetrators and victims were interlocked in the devilish game of cover-up and uncovering.

It is highly instructive to use Primo Levi as our Virgilian guide to this infernal game of cover-uncover.[13] He makes the point that the most solid materials for uncovering the facts of the crime are the memories of the survivors. But then he goes further and makes the point that the most useful accounts are those that were taken by the relatively more privileged inmates. Those who were needed for their technical skills, like electricians, were better off and less restricted in their movements and thus had a larger picture of life in the camps.

The ordinary inmates were too confined and too devastated to perceive the larger picture. Many of them did not even have a clue in which part of Europe they were being kept. Among the relatively privileged observers, Primo

Levi argues, the political prisoners were the more aware of their role as witnesses, seeing it as a political act. The best accounts about the camps came from them. They had better conditions in comparison to the Jews, they had a better view, they even had access to paper and pencil from time to time, and on occasion they had access to documents. Apart from Jews and criminals, they were also included among "the permanents," those who spent the longest terms in the camps. So the best historians of the camps came, Primo Levi claims, from among the political prisoners. But were they the best moral witnesses?

There is no question that the antifascist political witnesses were strongly morally motivated. It would be foolish to rob them of the title of moral witness just because they were also politically active. But then the political witness, though he or she can be a moral witness, is not the paradigm case of a moral witness. The ideal type of the political witness is one who believes that the incriminating evidence that she gathers is an instrument in the war effort. They are not just hoping that somewhere sometime there will be a moral community that will heed their story, but they hope that they are playing an active part in the very unfolding of the story.

A paradigmatic moral witness, on the other hand, is one who ascribes intrinsic value to his testimony, no matter what the instrumental consequences of it are going to be.

The political witness, by temperament and training, can be a much better witness than the mere moral witness for the structure of evil and not only for episodes of evil. And thus he can be a more valuable witness in uncovering the factual truth. The political witness can be very noble in fighting evil against all odds. And yet as an ideal type, although his features partly overlap with those of the moral witness, the political witness is still distinct, not to be confused with the moral witness. Both are engaged in uncovering what evil tries to cover up. The political witness may be more effective in uncovering the factual truth, in telling it like it was. But the moral witness is more valuable at telling it like it felt, that is, telling what it was like to be subjected to such evil. The first-person accounts of moral witnesses are essential to what they report, whereas political witnesses can testify from a third-person perspective without much loss.

The authority of the moral witness comes, among other things, from the ability to "describe *this*." The ability to describe does not preclude the idea that what the witness *expresses* is how "ineffable" the experience of radical evil is. One-way of expressing the ineffable is by recourse to describing the-moment-before and to the-moment-after the real horror takes place but avoiding the moment of horror itself. The Polish-Jewish writer Ida Fink is an outstanding moral witness who does just that.

Intriguing Cases

In his remarkable *Remarks on Frazer's Golden Bough*, Wittgenstein asks: "What makes human sacrifice something deep and sinister anyway? Is it only the suffering of the victims that impresses us in this way? No, this deep and sinister aspect is not obvious just from learning the history of the external action, but we impute it from an experience in ourselves."[14] The distinction Wittgenstein is trying to make is between two types of explanation, or rather between a historical (genetic, causal) explanation on the one hand and an elucidation of the meaning (significance, import) of symbolic behavior on the other.

In trying to understand a ritual of human sacrifice, it is not the historical account of how the ritual evolved that yields understanding but rather our grasp of the deep and sinister impression that the ritual makes on us. This kind of understanding is not gained by a mechanical enumeration of the dead or the badly injured but by an elucidatory description of what took place so that we can link the experience of the victims with our own meager experience.

I believe that Wittgenstein's distinction bears directly on our effort to delineate the role of the moral witness in *our* life. This is so in spite of the fact that Wittgenstein's elucidation has to do with symbolic behavior, whereas the experience with evil we are talking about is not symbolic.

What we expect from a moral witness is an elucidation of the dark and sinister character of human sacrifice and of the torture and humiliation inflicted by evil regimes. The moral witness is not necessarily at his best in giving a causal or functional account of the mechanism of evil. For that role, the political witness may be better.

I believe that the Committee for Truth and Reconciliation in South Africa rightly sensed that there is more to the apartheid experience than just telling the facts. They felt, I believe, the need for elucidation, but they used the wrong terms for it—"social truth," "narrative truth," "healing truth." These made truth, real truth, look like a very soft notion.

The authority of the moral witness has to do with his sincerity. That is, it has to do with a strong congruence between his emotions and his avowals, and with his not making concessions to himself. But sincerity is only part of it; authenticity is another. An authentic person is one who gets rid of all his personae (masks) and gives expression to his "true self," especially in the extreme circumstances of being unprotected by a civilized moral environment.

Some philosophers of authenticity welcomed extreme and trying circumstances as providing edifying experiences. It strikes me as obscene to welcome a Nazi concentration camp for providing opportunities for edifying experiences. This, however, is not to deny that among those who survived the camps were some who came out true to themselves, asked fundamental questions, and rejected suicide not just out of atavistic instincts but as an act of conscious defiance. And among those who rejected suicide, a few did so for the sake of becoming witnesses. This decision gave meaning to their lives. It is not right to view this decision as an expression of an existential fantasy of trying to play God by becoming a sort of *causa sui*. It is to be viewed as a deliberate effort to make one's life a life of self-definition under the most adverse conditions.

Among the self-defining features is the mission of telling your story, of living with a sense of being a witness. To be sure, living with the sense of being a witness can be a form of living under self-deception: you want to live, you cannot find a justification to carry on, and you tell yourself that you do it for the higher goal of being a witness. This form of useful bad faith—useful because it helps you to survive—is a form of inauthenticity. But the possibility of bad faith does not mean the impossibility of becoming a witness out of good faith.

Witness by Proxy

In 1929 Franz Werfel, while on tour in Damascus, met Armenian refugees who had escaped the great Turkish massacre and ended up in wretched conditions in Syria. Their story touched him deeply, and he took it upon himself to tell it. His book, *The Forty Days of Musa Dagh*, though confined to the Armenian settlements around Mount Moses, describes the plight of the Armenians in a way never done before and perhaps after.[15] Werfel's ability to describe it was partly due to genuine documents of the time and partly to his vivid imagination. The protagonist in the book is an Armenian spectator, Gabriel Baradian, who, after living in Paris for more than twenty years, comes to visit his family, only to find himself in a situation of acute crisis. The spectator turns into an actor.

Does Gabriel "go proxy" for Werfel, turning Werfel into a moral witness? No matter how strongly Werfel identifies with the Armenians, and how concretely he was able to depict the evil inflicted on them, he is no witness. One has to have some knowledge by acquaintance to be a witness, and his knowledge was entirely by description. This, I believe, is a necessary condition for being a moral witness. Now, *The Forty Days of Musa Dagh* came out in 1933, the year Franz Werfel himself came under Nazi persecution. Suppose that, contrary to fact, he had written his story of the Armenians after having some parallel experiences as a Jew victimized by the Nazis. Could this count as having the right experience for being a moral witness? My answer is still no. This experience might have enhanced the formidable empathy that he had anyway, but the authority of a moral witness comes from being an eye-witness.

Can there be a fake moral witness? The answer should be crystal clear: no. If Werfel's honest fictional account doesn't count as the testimony of a moral witness, what chance is there for a fake account that pretends to be nonfiction?

But then the case of Binjamin Wilkomirski (so-called) shows us how baffling true-to-life cases can be to our conceptual analysis. Bruno Grosjean was born to a single mother in the Swiss town of Biel. He was adopted by Dr. Kurt and Mrs. Martha Dössekker and assumed their last name. At a certain point in his life, he started to write his "memoirs" as a Jewish child in the terrible years of the war, claiming to have memories starting as a three-year-old in Majdanek, later in Auschwitz-Birkenau, and ending up in an orphanage in Krakow after the war. His memories of childhood from 1939 to 1948, published in 1995 under the title *Fragments* by Binjamin Wilkomirski, made a tremendous impression and were described by critics as "morally important" and "profoundly moving." Very few now believe his story. But then if you ask the opinion of the Holocaust researcher Israel Gutman, as did the essayist Elena Lappin, you are bound to be very intrigued indeed.[16]

Gutman himself lived through the experience of

Majdanek and Auschwitz. "He is not a fake," he says of Wilkomirski. "He is someone who lives this story very deeply in his soul. The pain is authentic." It is clear that Gutman doesn't think that Wilkomirski's story is true, though he hedges this by saying that extraordinary things happened in the Holocaust. But then he says: "I don't think it's that important. Wilkomirski has written a story he has experienced deeply, that's for sure. So that, even if he is not Jewish, the fact that he was so deeply affected by the Holocaust is of huge importance."[17]

I do not share Gutman's intuitions. I use *experience, authentic*, and *fake* as objective categories. A mere act of identification with children in the Holocaust does not establish identity as one of them. Experience means either a personal encounter or undergoing something "inner." Sometimes we tend to conflate the two. Especially with regard to a religious experience, we infer from undergoing a spiritual conversion the occurrence of an encounter with God. Under a charitable account, Wilkomirski underwent a spiritual act of identification, but he did not experience a personal encounter that is a necessary condition for being a witness, let alone a moral witness.

Is an autobiographical confession, like that of Augustine or Rousseau, the testimony of a moral witness? In these confessions the authors do not tell us about external evil but about the evil in their own soul. Augustine tells us about his trivial theft of pears. But he finds in it an experience of evil since he neither needed nor even fully ate the pears; the sole purpose of the theft was the theft itself.

Rousseau had a great deal more to confess. The revered author of Emil is none other than the man who handed over his five children, borne him by the simple woman Terèse, to an orphanage and utterly deserted them there. Jean-Jacques made all sorts of concessions to himself, and his confessions sound more like apologia than true repentance. But still, even as an act of attrition his confessions call for a great deal of courage. My concern, however, is not in evaluating his veracity. Though sincerity is not irrelevant for evaluating a moral witness, my main concern here is whether a confession, assuming it is true, is a testimonial of a moral witness.

I think that the relation of witnessing, like the relation of loving, is a nonreflexive relation, not an irreflexive relation like being taller than oneself. Some people love themselves and some do not, but no one is taller than himself. Likewise, it is possible, but not necessary, for one to witness oneself. It involves first-person knowledge of one's mental states, including one's evil states of mind. I do not therefore see a conceptual reason for disqualifying confessions from counting as moral testimony. Yet they do not constitute paradigmatic cases of what makes one into a moral witness. The paradigmatic case, to repeat, has to do with an encounter with external evil.

Testimony and Evidence

In many traditional societies being a formal witness in court means having a special status. Not everyone can be a witness, even if he (or, especially, if she) has relevant information to the case. Josephus writes that women in the time of the Bible were not eligible to testify in court, and the same was true for Roman women. The rationale might have been that there are categories of people, such as gamblers, who lack minimum respectability and so can damage the reputation of the court.

I believe, however, that respectability is not the whole story about the practice of banning certain categories of people from becoming formal witnesses. This practice goes with a certain image of truth. Truth in this image is something deep, not easily observed on the surface. Truth is not accessible to all, and important truth is esoteric and is due to revelation from special authorities. The convey-ing of truth calls for authority. One might say that the whole thrust of the Enlightenment and of the new science was to undermine the picture of truth as hidden depth.

In the "enlightened" picture, truth is given in principle

to all; truth is on the surface. Even expert scientific knowledge is not esoteric knowledge but is in principle knowledge open to all. In the final analysis, the authority of the "new knowledge" hinges only on observations. In this new picture, the reliability of hearsay testimony is tested by sampling the witness's statements against our observations.

In science the great divide is between theory and observation. Theory is tested by observation, and theory is our way of enlarging the scope of our knowledge beyond what we can observe directly. In the final analysis there is no arbiter of the validity of our theories except our observations, meager as they may be in comparison to the theory. The paradox is that on the one hand the division of labor and the degree of expertise that go into modern science are on a scale unknown in the past, and on the other hand we nevertheless claim that science is open to all.

The division between theory and observation is meant, among other things, to explain away this paradox. Modern theories are tested by highly sophisticated methods and by observations that are themselves theory-dependent. Testing is not all that different, in the level of skill it involves, from the construction of theories. But then the claim is that in *principle* the level of sophistication in the testing can be reduced to some raw levels of unsophisticated observations. In this picture, what should be sorted out is the relation between theoretical hypotheses and their observational evidence.

Our project of characterizing moral witnesses seems to go against the scientific trend of shifting the emphasis from the personal authority of the witness to the evidence itself. While we do not invest the moral witness with traditional authority, we seem to endow him with a special sort of charisma. The charisma comes from having a special kind of experience which is elevated to some sort of high spirituality that makes the witness a moral force.

The experience involved seems different from calm, methodical observation. Thus it seems that we take the moral witness to be closer to one who receives a revealed truth than to an eyewitness who observes, say, a crime. Our image of the moral witness invokes an aristocracy of suffering, not the democracy of giving evidence. Our critic might add that having been in a concentration camp should not be viewed as going through the ordeal of glowing iron to see who comes out of the experience unscathed. So far for the critic.

In Defense of the Idea of the Moral Witness

Two great forces in modern philosophy push for everybody's equal access to truth: observation and reason. Observation, the empiricists stress, is open to all those who are not distracted by motivational factors (the "will"). Reason, by which we can amplify our observed knowledge, is the ability to follow a reliable method for gaining knowledge. Our innate capacity for reasoning is enough to make us enlarge our limited restricted knowledge.

This picture seems to be confirmed by modern science as a triumph of accumulated knowledge, as against the traditional picture according to which a special witness, through the authority of the Scriptures, conveys knowledge. If we accept the idea that empirical knowledge gained through direct observation is the least problematic knowledge, we have to admit that the observational, first-hand knowledge that each of us has is exceedingly limited. When we draw on the observation of others, then we do not, strictly speaking, draw on observation anymore but on a hearsay account of the observations of others.

The expression "*our* observation" hides an important fact. I enlarge my own meager base of observation not by "induction" or "inference" or "proof" but mostly through the testimony of others which, in turn, usually consists not of what they directly observed but of what they themselves took on trust from others. This holds true even when we watch television. We depend on others to tell us that the fireworks we observed on the screen at the turn of the millennium occurred in Sydney, Australia. Testimony, not direct observation, is our basic source of evidence and knowledge, and the belief that it can be reduced to observation plus induction or deduction cannot be defended.

There is no way that I can check the testimony of others by my own limited observational resources. I have to count on others for such checks, which means that I am dependent on their testimonials. The idea that I am able to check, in stages and in a way recursively, strikes me as a fantasy.

If this line of thinking is right, and I believe it is, it has a very important implication for our lives.[18] *We are dependent on testimonials in an essential way.* This is true for all our walks of life: science, religion, history, court, and of course for our collective memory. In my picture, it is not the case that I am caught in a web of beliefs such that the peripheral ones are observational and they have to be matched with observational reports. Rather, I am caught in a network of witnesses. Some I take on trust because of the thick relations that I have with them—my parents, for instance. My trust in them can serve me badly. They can, with the best of intentions, inject me with prejudices, superstitions, mistakes, and indoctrination of bad ideologies and wrong values. But usually if they do it they do it because they themselves are deluded, not because they want to misguide me. In this view, my attitude toward a potential witness often is prior to my attitude toward her testimony. My belief *in* (her) is prior to my belief *that* (what she says is true) and cannot be reduced to the latter. I may in due course change my attitude to my witnesses, add some, and drop others. But this is a slow and painful process that has as much to do with loyalties as with epistemology.

In general my witnesses address me as much in writing as in speaking. They write books and publish in newspapers. I do not know most of my witnesses first-hand, and yet I count on them constantly. And I am quite sure that what I describe here with regard to myself holds true for you too. In short, witnesses and testimonies are the most crucial way for us to acquire knowledge. Witnesses are vital not just for enlarging the scope of observational knowledge but even more for elucidating the significance of human actions, symbolic acts, and language itself. So my main claim is that our knowledge forces us to create a hierarchy of witnesses, indeed to create many hierarchies: different people we trust and mistrust with respect to different things. This should not offend our democratic instincts. The democratic remedy for the hierarchies of witnesses is not to deny this fact but to break the traditional monopoly of just one elite of witnesses. But democracy is not my concern here.

How does all this tie in with moral witnesses? Well, although all sufferers of evil are equal in being qualified to attest to their suffering, they are far from equal in their ability to elucidate their experience of evil to us who were not there. This is a great achievement that should not be scorned because it may offend an alleged democratic instinct about witnesses.

A Moral Witness or an Ethical Witness

Given my distinction between ethics and morality as based on the distinction between thick and thin relations (ethics informs our thick relations, morality our thin relations), let me ask, Is what I have here called a moral witness really a *moral* witness or perhaps an *ethical* witness? My answer is, he or she is both. The concern with evil as an attack on the very idea of a moral system is indeed a moral concern par excellence. On the other hand, the moral witness as a "witness to the common lot" is most effective and authentic when he or she speaks for the "lot" of victims with a thick identity based on thick relations among them. A moral witness may well give voice to an ethical community that is endangered by an evil force. So I conclude that we should take the adjective *moral* in the expression *moral witness* as systematically ambiguous between ethics and morality.

6

FORGIVING AND FORGETTING

Humanistic Orientation

WHAT IS THE relation between forgiving and forgetting? In this chapter I will try to answer this question by first uncovering the religious underpinnings of these two concepts. I believe that the notion of forgiveness is deeply rooted in religion, and I believe that uncovering these roots is a necessary preliminary step before we can tackle their conceptual analysis. Still, my ethics and morality are humanistic, not religious. This means that the sources of their justification lie in humans, and not in any "higher" beings.

I take humanism, however, to consist of two claims and not just one: first, that human beings are the *only* source of justification for ethics and morality; second, that humans are a *sufficient* source for the justification of ethics and morality. I agree with the first claim but not with the second: I believe that human beings are the only source of justification but that this source is not sufficient. The importance of religious ethics is in its negative lesson, in making us aware of our lack of sufficient sources of justification.

We live with insufficient sources to justify our ethics and morality. Our situation is not unlike that of David Hume's followers, who believe that only deduction can sufficiently justify an empirical claim but that all we have is induction. It may very well be the case here that we need a distinction between justifying *to* and justifying *that*. While we may have full justification that will satisfy those to whom we try to justify our beliefs and actions, we may still lack satisfactory reasons that such-and-such is the case or that so-and-so is to be done. So lacking sufficient justification for ethics or morality means lacking sufficient justification *that* but not necessarily sufficient justification *to*.[1]

The Genealogy of Forgiving and Forgetting

Our concepts of sin, forgiveness, and forgetting are rooted in religious picture. By picture I mean a collection of familiar objects that can provide a metaphorical model for the problematical concept. The expressions that describe a picture are "dead" metaphors whose metaphorical quality escapes their users. Users are in the grip of the picture if they are not aware of its metaphorical nature and cannot think of any alternative way of saying what the picture expresses. The protest, "But how else could it be?" is the hallmark of being in such a grip.

Thus, for example, the idea of sin as a bloodstain and of purification and atonement as the removal of the stain form a powerful picture in the Bible. In the verse, "Though your sins are scarlet, they may become white as snow" (Isaiah 1:18), the metaphorical nature of the picture is quite clear, but in the verses, "There is blood on your hands; wash yourselves and be clean. Put away the evil of your deeds" (Isaiah 1:15–16), the picture takes over and the metaphorical quality of the washing disappears. Witnessing the hold of the hand-washing picture on Lady Macbeth ("A little water clears us of this deed") is enough to convince us how difficult it is to escape the grip of this metaphor.[2]

The Bible uses the Hebrew word *salakh*, meaning forgive, only for God's forgiveness. It does not use it for one person's forgiving another, as is the case in modern Hebrew. The prevalent word used in the Bible for the latter purpose is *nasa*, meaning "to bear" or "to carry." This term is interesting because it presents an alternative picture of the sin as a heavy burden. The forgiver shares the sinner's burden of sin. Unlike the Hebrew root *salakh*, which may have originally meant "to wash," the idea of bearing a sin presents a totally different picture.

But human beings do not bear the burdens of sin alone. God too can bear the sins of individuals, as in the psalmist's declaration, "You have borne the iniquity of my sin" (Psalms 32:5, my literal translation), or of the collective, as the psalmist continues, "You have borne the sin of your people" (Psalms 85:3, again in my literal translation). Yet it is not only human beings and God who can carry iniquities. The burden can also be carried by the scapegoat: "The goat shall carry all their iniquities upon itself into some barren waste" (Leviticus 16:22).

Wittgenstein makes the following remarks about the ritual of the Day of Atonement. On that day the High Priest places the sins of the Israelites on the goat and sends it into the wilderness. "The scapegoat on which one lays one's sins, and who runs away into the desert with them — a false picture similar to those which cause errors in philosophy." What is misleading in the image of the scapegoat? Why does Wittgenstein, in spite of his high regard for mythology, see the scapegoat as a bad myth? Bad myths are made up of superstitions, that is, of beliefs about supernatural causal mechanisms. Bad philosophy, that is, metaphysics, is also based on this sort of superstition. In any case the picture of the scapegoat suggests the-

urgist magic—the art of compelling the gods in some supernatural causal way to do what the magician wants
them to do, in this case to displace human sins onto the
head of the goat.

The problem in Wittgenstein's view is not the actual
use of magic, provided the magic action or religious ritual is conceived only as the expression of a wish to be
cleansed of sin. But when it expresses a belief in the
causal efficacy of the action, then it creates a bad picture:
"Baptism as washing—there is a mistake only if magic is
presented as science."[3] When the action does not merely
express a desire for purification but is seen as *causing*
purification, it becomes a superstition.

What else is bad about the picture of a goat carrying
human iniquities? It is not the crudeness of the picture
that bothers Wittgenstein. On the contrary, when some of
these images are refined they may be more misleading
than in their crude state. What bothers him is not that a
picture is crude but that it is vague. This means that the
associations arising from it are confused and confusing.

In the case of the scapegoat, the picture is misleading
because we tie the wrong emotions to it. A goat is not an
appropriate model for the forgiveness of sin because it is
not a creature that we see as expressing innocence, even if
it actually is an innocent creature. The "servant of God"
of whom Isaiah says "The Lord laid upon him the guilt of

us all" is compared not to a goat but to a lamb or a ewe. These are animals that, unlike the goat, are seen as representing innocence. One must separate the sheep from the goats. The scapegoat has entered Western culture as a creature that people blame and punish for sins it did not commit—sins that were actually committed by those doing the blaming and the punishing. But the scapegoat, even if totally blameless, is not a symbol of innocence. It generally represents radical otherness—the different, the totally strange and threatening. This is why it is so easy to place blame and sin on it. This change in the picture of the scapegoat upon entering Western culture is not a coincidence. It shows that the goat was always a bad model for the idea of forgiveness and carrying sins.

There are thus two different levels on which we test a picture. One is the cognitive level: Does it represent or strengthen illusions? The other is the emotive level: Is it linked to appropriate feelings? The picture of the scapegoat fails both tests.

Forgiveness: Blotting Out the Sin or Covering It Up?

Two religious models of sin and forgiveness still permeate the concept of forgiveness in present-day humanistic morality: forgiveness as blotting out the sin, and forgiveness as covering it up. Blotting out a sin means forgetting it absolutely. Covering it up means disregarding it without forgetting it. When the psalmist asks God to "wash me, that I may become whiter than snow" (Psalms 51:7), the meaning of his request is immediately clarified: "Blot out all my guilt" (51:9). In the blotting out model, forgiving is manifested as forgetting. Jeremiah puts it clearly, "For I will forgive their wrongdoing and remember their sin no more" (31:34).

The one who forgives and forgets is God, since it is only against Him that we sin ("Against thee, thee only, I have sinned" Psalms 51:4). Sin estranges man—both the individual and the collective—from God. This estrangement is expressed as forgetting: "The Lord has forsaken me; my God has forgotten me" (Isaiah 49:14). But God does not easily forget. "Can a woman forget the infant at her breast, or a loving mother the child of her womb? Even these forget, yet I will not forget you" (49:15).

The comparison between the God who remembers man and the mother who remembers the child of her womb is interesting. In Hebrew the words *rehem* (womb) and *rahamim* (mercy) stem from the same root. Mercy is returning those who are far away to their source, the womb. Hence, the act of remembering is an act of mercy and grace.

Forgetting thus plays a double role—forgetting the person who has sinned, and forgetting the sin itself. This double role is connected with another important biblical image of sin and forgiveness—the Divine book. This book is sometimes seen as containing the names of those who are destined to live, as opposed to those who are blotted out because of their sins (that is, doomed to oblivion). After the Israelites sinned with the Golden Calf, Moses pleaded with God, "If thou wilt forgive them, forgive. But if not, blot out my name, I pray, from thy book which thou hast written" (Exodus 32:32). And god answered, "It is the man who has sinned against me that I will blot out from my book" (32:33).

There are actually two conceptions of the Divine book. One is that of an account book in which sins are written on the debit side: "All is on record before me; I will not keep silence; I will repay your iniquities" (Isaiah 65:6). This account book lists deeds on both the credit side and the debit side. The other conception is of a book that contains a list of names. The names of those who are destined to live appear on the list, while the names of those who have been condemned to die are blotted out: "Let them be blotted out from the book of life and not be enrolled among the righteous" (Psalms 69:28). In Divine bookkeeping, sins are listed as liabilities and good deeds as assets. Those whose balance is positive are listed in the book of life.

The plea for forgiveness is thus a plea for forgetting in

the sense of blotting out liabilities. This picture of forgiveness is expressed most clearly in the New Testament (Matthew 6:12), where the Greek verb for forgiveness is a word meaning canceling a debt (*afinmai*). And so is the parable of the slave who refused to forgive, which comes as an answer to Peter's question, "How oft shall my brother sin against me, and I forgive him? Till seven times?" (Matthew 18:21). The master cancelled the debt of the slave, but the slave refused to cancel the debt owed to him by a fellow slave. "I forgave thee all the debt, because thou desiredst me. Shouldest not thou also have had compassion on thy fellow servant?" (18:32–33), says the Master when he hears about the slave's refusal.

There are thus four different pictures of forgiveness in the Bible: as carrying a burden, as covering up, as blotting out, and as canceling a debt. The first three pictures can be seen as progressively increasing degrees of forgiveness, as expressed in the literal translation of Psalms 32:1–2, bearing one's transgression, covering up one's sin, and not taking one's sin into account—ceasing to hold one guilty. The fourth picture, of forgiveness as canceling a debt, can be interpreted on any one of these levels: bearing part of the debt, ignoring the debt even though it still exists, or wiping it out completely. It seems to me that there is an opposition between forgiveness as covering up and as blotting out the sin. This opposition is the difference between the ideas of forgiving and forgetting. I shall return to an evaluation and critique of these two pictures below.

Forgiving as an Attitude and as a Duty

Forgiving means overcoming anger and vengefulness. This is so with regard to the God of the Bible: "Compassionately, however, he forgave their guilt instead of killing them, repeatedly repressing his anger instead of rousing his full wrath" (Psalms 78:38). But overcoming anger and vengefulness can also take place without forgiveness. Jacob did Esau wrong, cheating him of their father's blessing. As a result, "Esau bore a grudge against Jacob" (Genesis 27:41) and planned revenge: "The time of mourning for my father will soon be here; then I will kill my brother Jacob (27:42). When Rebecca, the mother of Jacob and Esau, heard of this, she warned her beloved son Jacob to stay away "until your brother's anger cools. When it has subsided and he forgets what you have done to him, I will send and fetch you back" (27:44–45). The way Rebecca believes that Esau will overcome his anger and his drive for revenge is not by forgiving Jacob but by forgetting his deed. She knows that Esau is quick to anger, and therefore takes care to give his anger a chance to cool, so that over time he will forget what has happened. Esau's overcoming of his anger and vengefulness is thus not an act of forgiveness, which would have moral significance (or ethical, for that matter).

If it occurs through simple forgetfulness, it is not real forgiveness. Forgiveness is a conscious decision to change one's attitude and to overcome anger and vengefulness. Forgetfulness may in the last analysis be the most effective method of overcoming anger and vengefulness, but since it is an omission rather than a decision, it is not forgiveness. But then, like in the case of remembering, there is an indirect way by which forgiveness as a decision can bring about forgetting and thereby complete the process of forgiveness. The decision to forgive makes one stop brooding on the past wrong, stop telling it to other people, with the end result of forgetting it or forgetting that it once mattered to you greatly. Such a case of forgetting should matter a great deal both morally and ethically.

Forgiveness as a Gift

In the Hebrew bible there is no duty to forgive. The New Testament does contain an explicit exhortation to forgive: "For if you forgive others the wrongs they have done, your heavenly Father will also forgive you; but if you do not forgive others, then the wrongs you have done will not be forgiven by your Father" (Matthew 6:14–15). The idea is that there is no one who does not need forgiveness: "The world contains no man so righteous that he can do right always and never do wrong" (Ecclesiastes 7:20).

And even if the individual did not sin personally, he or she still needs forgiveness due to original sin. Since "one misdeed was the condemnation for all men" (Romans 5:18), we are all sinners, or at least we are all in a state of guilt. We all need forgiveness, and so we must all be capable of forgiving. This is the view of the New Testament.

Maimonides states the requirement of forgiveness as follows: "It is forbidden to be obdurate and not allow oneself to be appeased. On the contrary, one should be easily pacified and find it difficult to become angry. And, when asked by an offender for forgiveness, one should forgive with a sincere mind and willing spirit. Even if one had been much vexed and grievously wronged, he is not to avenge nor bear a grudge."[4] This is a forceful exhortation to forgive, which places an obligation on the person who was wronged to forgive the offender when the latter is sincerely repentant. The passage gives the impression that forgiveness is not an act of loving kindness but a moral religious duty.

I believe that the present-day humanistic morality of duty has made it difficult to imagine combining duty with loving kindness. Forgiveness is not supererogatory—beyond the call of duty—in the sense that whoever forgives is praiseworthy but whoever does not is not blameworthy.

Religious moral duties are like the duties that exist in societies with a well-developed institution of gift exchange. It would seem that the very idea of a gift as something that is bestowed gratuitously does not fit in with a normative expectation for compensation with a counter gift. For then how do gift exchanges differ from economic transactions?

This question has vexed many anthropologists from the time of Marcel Mauss. I do not have a simple answer to offer. A more complex answer will have to include at least one central component: gifts are intended to form or strengthen social ties between the original giver and the one who returns a gift. Economic transactions are intended to provide goods and services for utilitarian purposes. Hence a central aspect of gift-giving is often the nonutilitarian nature of the gift, such as its decorative function.

In the Bible, gifts to others and offerings to God are both denoted by the same word *minha*. And there is indeed a clear element of gift exchange in the offerings to God in the Hebrew bible. The idea I want to propose here is that the duties involved in forgiveness, both those of the one who asks for it and those of the one who bestows it, are similar to the duties involved in exchanging gifts. The purpose in both cases has to do with the nature of the personal relationship that existed before the offense occurred. But there remains a difference. Forgiveness, unlike ordinary gifts, is not intended to form or strengthen a relationship but rather to restore it to its previous state.

Rejecting a sincere plea for forgiveness is like rejecting a gift. A weighty justification is needed in both cases. Consider this famous case: "The day came when Cain brought some of the produce of the soil as a gift to the Lord; and Abel brought some of the first-born of his flock, the fat portions of them. The Lord received Abel and his gift with favor; but Cain and his gift he did not receive. Cain was very angry and his face fell" (Genesis 4:3–5). The traditional Jewish Bible commentators felt that gifts should not be rejected arbitrarily. The rejection of a gift needs to be justified. Gifts impose obligations: the obligation to accept the gift unless there is good reason to reject it, and also the obligation to return a gift in a gift-exchange society. I am claiming that the obligation to forgive, to the extent that such an obligation exists, is like the obligation not to reject a gift—an obligation not to reject the expression of remorse and the plea for forgiveness.

As we have seen, the religious context of sin and forgiveness suggests a variety of pictures of how sins can be forgiven or forgotten. The most important pictures for our purposes are those of blotting out and covering up. The metaphor of blotting out depicts forgiving as absolutely forgetting the sinful act. Forgiveness restores the personal relationship between the offender and the offended to where it was before the offence took place. The metaphor of covering up, in contrast, suggests disregarding the offence without forgetting it. Traces of the sinful offense remain, but the offended party does not retaliate by taking revenge against the one who wronged him.

When we are dissatisfied with something we have written, there are two ways of getting rid of it: deleting it or crossing it out. In deletion the written material is totally erased, while crossing out leaves traces of the error under the crossing-out line. Blotting out is analogous to deleting; covering up is like crossing out. I shall argue that the image of covering up is conceptually, psychologically, and morally preferable to the picture of blotting out—that it is better to cross out than to delete the memories of an offense. In short, I argue that forgiveness is based on disregarding the sin rather than forgetting it.

Returning

The religious person asking for forgiveness hopes for the erasure of the sin. He prays that God will undo the past. This wish for the past to be undone has even infiltrated the secular notion of forgiveness, in the form of a plea for the absolute obliteration of the evil that was committed. As long as what is involved is only the wish of the person seeking forgiveness, there is nothing wrong with a wish.

But when it is accompanied by a magical belief that the past can be undone through atonement, this is an illusion. There is a good reason why Calvinism was so adamantly opposed to the very idea of forgiveness, since it saw this as an attempt to manipulate the Divinity. The Calvinist notion of predestination was intended to affirm a sovereign Divinity whose will cannot be influenced by magical manipulations or by the "emotional blackmail" of penitence.

The central metaphor is not erasure but, rather, returning. The sinner who has become distanced from God because of his sin now returns to Him. The first step in correcting the wrongdoing is not God's forgiveness but the sinner's act of returning to God.

The first penitent was Cain: "Cain said to the Lord, 'My sin is too great to bear!'" (Genesis 4:13). God partially forgives Cain. He does not enact the judicial principle that a murderer must be punished by death: "Expiation cannot be made on behalf of the land for blood shed on it except by the blood of the man that shed it" (Numbers 35:33). But God's forgiveness of Cain does not involve erasing his sin. On the contrary, the way in which God protects Cain is to "put a mark on him, in order that anyone meeting him should not kill him" (Genesis 4:15). The mark of Cain has turned into a haunting picture of the mark of the criminal (indeed of the murderer) that cannot be erased.

The mark of Cain highlights the tension between forgiveness and memory. Forgiveness that involves a mark of Cain is not total forgetting.

Repentance in the Hebrew bible has several components: remorse, confession, fasting, prayer, and even some customs related to bereavement such as tearing one's clothes and wearing sackcloth. This is, for example, how King David acted when he repented for his sin with Bathsheba (2 Samuel 12). Of all these components, the most crucial one is remorse. The question is why should remorse be considered a reason for forgiveness, and why is remorse so essential in reestablishing the relationship between the forgiver and the offender?

Remorse offers us a nonmagical way of undoing the past. Although it is impossible to undo what has been done, since the past cannot be changed, it is possible to change our interpretation of the past. By expressing remorse the offender presents himself in a new light, a light that can be projected into the past. His ability to feel remorse attests that he is not basically evil, even if the act that he performed was abominable. The sinner does not deny the badness of his deed, as then he would not be expressing remorse, but his very assumption of responsibility for the deed is supposed to create a rift between the act and the doer. Thus, an offender can be forgiven even if the offense cannot be forgotten. In this view, remorse accords with the idea that forgiveness is not tantamount to the obliteration of the sin.

These remarks about the role of remorse in correcting the wrongdoing show why I prefer the picture of covering up the sin to the picture of blotting it out. Remorse does not involve the magic of an atonement offering.

There is a sense in which the blotting-out image is incoherent. If it is necessary to forget the sin totally in order to forgive, we are faced with a contradiction. It is like Philip Roth's injunction: "Remember to forget." This is discussed in the following section.

Can Forgetting Be Intentional?

As I mentioned already, we have no trouble distinguishing voluntary from involuntary muscles. The test of whether a muscle is voluntary is whether I can make it work on demand just like that, directly and immediately, without the mediation of any other muscles. Leg muscles are voluntary; heart muscles are not. I can obviously cause my heart to beat faster by starting to run, but this does not meet the criterion of a voluntary muscle.

Fakirs are supposed to be able to make all their muscles voluntary through practice. This would mean that the distinction between voluntary and involuntary muscles is empirical rather than conceptual. But we need not be concerned with fakirs, because we do not particularly care for our present purposes whether the difficulty of making an involuntary muscle work is a conceptual or an empirical one.

It would seem that the distinction between voluntarily and involuntary applies to mental acts as well. I can voluntarily think of a white elephant, but I cannot follow the instruction not to think of a white elephant. Forgetting cannot be voluntary. Just as I cannot voluntarily avoid thinking of a white elephant. I cannot decide to forget something just like that. And so if forgiving involves forgetting, it would seem that one could not decide to forgive. Forgiveness would not be a coherent concept. What then is forgiveness?

Members of a jury often hear evidence that is inadmissible and that they are not supposed to know about. If the judge asks the jurors to forget this evidence, this request would merely guarantee that they would remember it. Then what should the judge actually tell the jury? The judge generally instructs the jury that they must disregard the inadmissible evidence and that they must not make use of it as a reason for their verdict. The judge cannot request that the information not influence the jurors, but he can ask them not to use it as part of their justification of the verdict.

At first glance, it would seem that this is all we can ask

in the case of forgiveness as well. That is, all we can ask is that the one who was wronged should not take the offense into consideration as a reason for future behavior toward the offender. Forgiveness is the decision that the injury is not "admissible evidence," that it is no longer a reason for action. We have not offered any reason why the offended one should consider the injury as "inadmissible evidence"; that will come later. The matter we are discussing now is solely the question of what constitutes forgiveness. And the answer to this question stresses that forgiveness is the product of a voluntary decision in the practical realm.

Forgiveness in this sense is an example of what Joseph Raz calls "exclusionary reason"—that is, "a reason against acting for certain reasons."[5] In our case, forgiveness is an exclusionary reason against acting on reasons that rely on the injury to the forgiver committed by the offender. Forgiveness, then, is like a promise that commits us to disregard certain reasons for action.

According to this interpretation, "I forgive you" is a performative act, just like "I promise." And the act that is performed is that of undertaking a commitment to refrain from using certain reasons—in the case of forgiveness, reasons that are supposed to justify hostile or cold behavior toward the person who caused us injury.

Thus, forgiveness is first and foremost a policy: a policy of adopting an exclusionary reason with regard to someone who has wronged us. This view is compatible with the covering-up picture rather than with the blotting-out picture. To disregard is a decision, to forget is not. Therefore, forgiveness, which is voluntary, should not be tied to forgetting, which is involuntary. If forgiveness is really a decision to adopt a certain policy, then this view has a conceptual as well as a psychological advantage. The conceptual advantage is that it does not require us to do something that is involuntary; the psychological advantage is that while the request to forget makes remembering more likely, the request to disregard does not.

Forgiveness

The antithesis is that forgiveness is not a policy or decision but a change in the mental state of the one who was wronged ("a change of heart"). Forgetting the injury is part of what is required for this change of heart and for successful forgiveness. Since forgetting is not voluntary, neither is forgiveness. So forgiveness cannot be a voluntary mental act but is at best a mental change.

In other words, I cannot decide to forgive just like that, any more than I can decide to forget—and for more or less the same reasons. Instead, when I do forgive I undergo a shift in my mental state. Note, however, that this fact is not an argument against appeal to an indirect method of forgiveness any more than it is an argument against forgetting. Strengthening one's heart muscles through exercise is the result of a decision, even though it is not a direct decision to voluntarily activate one's heart muscles. The same is true of forgiving and forgetting. Both require an indirect approach.

At any rate, according to this view, forgiveness as "a change of heart" is not a policy. It is not even the policy of adopting an exclusionary reason. Such a policy is appropriate for a pardon but not for forgiveness. Forgiveness, in this view, is a matter of psychology, not of policy.

There are indeed biblical images of God, in the role of a judge or a king, forgiving people. In these cases, forgiveness is merely pardon: God disregards the sin in the narrow sense of not punishing the sinner. But when Jeremiah's God says to the Israelites, "I remember the unfailing devotion of your youth, the love of your bridal days, when you followed me in the wilderness" (2:2), he is not exercising forgiveness as pardon. Instead, it is forgiveness in the sense of a restoration of remembered intimacy that was lost because of the sin of later betrayal.

Forgiveness of this sort is not a policy but rather a case of overcoming resentment and vengefulness, of mastering anger and humiliation. Such overcoming is a result of a long effort rather than a decision to do something on the spot. We can compare it to overcoming smoking. True, one can indeed stop smoking just like that. But one cannot end one's desire to smoke just like that. This desire can be modified only gradually.

The word *forgiveness* denotes both a process and an achievement, just as the word *work* denotes both the process of working and the work that is accomplished. The forgiver makes a conscious decision at least in paradigmatic cases to enter a process whose end-result is forgetting the injury and restoring his relationship with the offender as though the injury had never occurred.

The decision to forgive is a decision to act in disregard of the injury. But as long as the offended one retains any scars from the injury, the forgiveness is not complete. Only the decision to begin this process is voluntary; the end-result of complete forgiveness is not voluntary any more than forgetting is, and so it cannot be guaranteed. There are elements of forgetting that can be voluntary, such as the decision not to brood over the injury, but forgetting itself is involuntary.

Total forgiveness entails forgetting—that is, blotting out rather than covering up. The initial decision to forget, however, does require remembering, otherwise the forgiveness has no meaning. "Natural" forgetting of an injury is not forgiveness and has no moral value. But the ideal end-result of forgiveness is the restoration of the original relationship between the offender and the forgiver, and this can ideally be achieved only when the forgiver does not feel any resentment or desire to avenge the injury.

Forgiveness as a policy touches upon the reasons for the decision to disregard the injury, but forgiveness as overcoming means mastering motives such as resentment and vengefulness that stem, whether consciously or not, from the injury itself. Forgiveness in the perhaps unattainable ideal sense is overcoming all traces and scars of the act to be forgiven. But this is God's blotting-out forgiveness rather than the human covering-up forgiveness.

Second-Order Forgiveness

And now for the synthesis: If the notion of overcoming resentment is properly understood, then forgiveness as a policy does not contradict the idea of forgiveness as overcoming resentment. This is because overcoming resentment does not require forgetting.

When we have been seriously wronged, we are liable to develop resentment against the one who wronged us. The decision to forgive is an expression of a second-order desire not to act upon our first-order feelings of resentment or vengefulness. This does not mean that the first-order sense of resentment or desire for revenge has disappeared, but only that the second-order desire has won. We do not act on our resentment or vengefulness. We do not forget, but we do forgive.

Yet I believe that we do not forgive out of a duty toward the offender. There is no general justification in my view for the duty to forgive out of some right that the offender has over us. Not even in cases when we recognize sincere repentance. We do not in general owe forgiveness to others, but we may owe it to ourselves (or, if you like, we may have such a duty to ourselves). This duty stems from not wanting to live with feelings of resentment and the desire for revenge. Those are poisonous attitudes and states of mind.

Indeed, there is a deeper point here that has to do with my notion of ethics. Ethics for me is primarily concerned with the way we should conduct our behavior and attitudes toward those with whom we have thick relations and about whom we are meant to care. Unless we are self-haters, we care about ourselves. So in my account ethics includes, as a special case, also this reflexive relation that one has with one's self. To the extent that forgiveness is an ethical duty, it is a duty in that special case of ethics, namely, a duty to ourselves.

Those who, on religious or on secular grounds, believe that there is an obligation to forgive in cases of genuine repentance are still facing Karamazov's question: Are there any unforgivable acts? If a torturer takes a woman's son and gives him to his dog to be torn to pieces, should the mother ever forgive the murder? Ivan Karamazov believes that she ought not to forgive. Indeed, even in my very meager notion of obligation to forgive as an obligation to oneself, not to the tormentor, it sounds hollow if not hideous to say to the mother that she ought to forgive for her own sake. What about telling her, "You must forget if you can, for the sake of carrying on with your life." This adage may be psychologically hollow, but it is by no means hideous.

There is no general *duty* to forget, not even in the truncated sense of duty to ourselves, since who we are depends on our not forgetting things that happened and that are important in our lives. But the role of memory in constituting who we are and what agents we are is in tension with the ideal of successful forgiveness as that which ends in forgetting the wrong done to us.

I maintain that what is needed for successful forgiveness is not forgetting the wrong done but rather overcoming the resentment that accompanies it. It is like forgetting an emotion in the sense of not reliving it when memory of the event comes to mind.

The right model for forgiving, both psychologically and ethically, is the covering-up model, not the blotting-out model. What ought to be blotted out is the memory of the emotion in the sense of reliving it, not in the sense of remembering it.

My last remarks refer to the end-result of a successful course of forgiveness. But the end-result of such a course is not in our hands. Only its beginning is up to us. It depends on two elements. The first is adopting, as a policy of behavior, an exclusionary reason to counter reasons for action that are based on the injury done to us. The second element is a second-order desire to overcome our first-order resentment, vengefulness, and insult stemming from that injury.

NOTES

Introduction

1. Sigmund Freud, *The Complete Psychological Works of Sigmund Freud*, trans. James Strachey (London: Hogarth Press, 1974), vol. 11, pp. 16–17.
2. Ralph Inge, *Philosophy of Plotinus*, Lecture 22 (1923).
3. Norman Malcolm, *Memory and Mind* (Ithaca: Cornell University Press, 1977).

1. Intensive Care

I owe the title of this chapter to the late poet Dennis Silk.

1. Joseph Brodsky, *Collected Poems in English* (New York: Farrar Strauss Giroux, 2000), p. 85.
2. David Edgar, *Pentecost* (London: Nick Hern Books, 1995).
3. My quotations from the Bible throughout the book

make use of various translations (as I judged them adequate).

4. Saul Kripke, *Naming and Necessity* (Cambridge: Harvard University Press, 1980).

5. Clifford Geertz, *The Interpretation of Cultures* (New York: Basic Books, 1973), pp. 369–380.

6. Miguel de Unamuno, trans. J. E. Crawford Flitch, *Tragic Sense of Life* (New York: Dover, 1954), p. 55.

7. Benedict Anderson, *Imagined Communities: Reflections on the Origins and Spread of Nationalism* (London: Verso, 1983).

8. Anna Akhmatova, *Poems of Akhmatova*, trans. Stanley Kunitz with Max Hayward (New York: A Mariner Book, Houghton Company, 1967), p. 99.

9. Harry Frankfurt, *The Importance of What We Care About* (Cambridge: Cambridge University Press, 1998), pp. 80–95. Harry Frankfurt, *Necessity, Volition, and Love* (Cambridge: Cambridge University Press, 1999), pp. 155–180.

10. Carol Gilligan, *In a Different Voice* (Cambridge: Harvard University Press, 1982).

11. Martin Heidegger, *Being and Time*, Trans. John Macquarrie and Edward Robinson (Oxford: Blackwell, 1962), p. 236.

12. Bernard Williams, *Ethics and the Limits of Philosophy* (Cambridge: Cambridge University Press, 1985), chaps. 8–9.

13. Sifra K'dushim 2,4 Midrash for Leviticus.

14. Moses Mendelssohn, trans. Allan Arkush, *Jerusalem* (Hanover and London: Brandies University Press, 1983), p. 102.

15. Immanual Kant, *The Metaphysics of Morals*, trans. Mary Gregor (Cambridge: Cambridge University Press, 1991), pt. 2, sec. 30.

16. David Hume, *A Treatise of the Human Nature* (Oxford: Clarendon Press), p. 581. See also Edward Royzman and Rahul Kumar, "On the relative preponderance of empathic sorrow and its relation to commonsense morality," *New Ideas in Psychology* 19 (2001): 131–144.

17. Peter Winch, *Trying to Make Sense* (Oxford: Blackwell, 1987).

2. Past Continuous

1. Jon Elster, *Solomonic Judgments: Studies in the Limitations of Rationality* (Cambridge: Cambridge University press, 1989), chap. 4. See also Jon Elster, *Ulysses Unbound* (Cambridge: Cambridge University Press, 2000), chap. 2, p. 12.

2. Eugene Winogrod and Ulric Neisser, eds., *Affect and Accuracy in Recall: Studies of "Flashbulb" Memories* (Cambridge: Cambridge University Press, 1992). See also Martin Conway, *Flashbulb Memories* (East Sussex: Lawrence Erlbaum, 1995).

3. R. Brown and J. Kulick, "Flashbulb Memories," *Cognition* 5: (1997): 73–99.

4. Edna Ullmann—Margalit, "The Generalization Argument: Where Does the Obligation Lie?" *Journal of Philosophy* 73 (1976): 511–522.

5. Max Weber, *The Protestant Ethic and the Spirit of Capitalism*, trans. Talcott Parsons (London: Allen & Unwin, 1930).

6. Moshe Halbertal and Avishai Margalit, *Idolatry*, trans. Naomi Goldblum (Cambridge: Harvard University Press, 1991), chap. 3.

7. George Mosse, *Fallen Soldiers: Reshaping the Memory of the World Wars* (New York: Oxford University Press, 1990), p. 75. George Mosse, *The Crisis of German Ideology: Intellectual Origins of the Third Reich* (New York: Grosset & Dunlap, 1964).

8. Thomas Scanlon, *What We Owe Each Other* (Cambridge: Harvard University Press, 1998).

9. Peter Kropotkin, *Mutual Aid: A Factor of Evolution* (London: Heineman, 1992).

10. Julia Kristeva, *Strategy to Ourselves* (New-York: Columbia University Press, 1991).

11. John Milton, *Paradise Lost*, ed. John Leonard (London: Penguin Books, 2000), bk. 1, lines 120–130.

12. Immanuel Kant, *Religion within the Limits of Reason Alone*, trans. T. M. Green and H. H. Hudson (New York: Harper and Brothers, 1960), bks. 1 and 3.

3. The Kernel

1. Avishai Margalit, *The Decent Society*, trans. Naomi Goldblum (Cambridge: Harvard University Press, 1996).
2. Edna Ullmann-Margalit and Sidney Morgenbesser, "Picking and Choosing," *Social Research* 44, no. 4 (1977): 757–758.
3. Russell Hardin, "Social identity," in *International Encyclopedia of the Social and Behavioral Sciences*, ed. Neil J. Smelser and Paul B. Baltes (New York: Elsevier, 2001), vol. 11, p. 7167.
4. Allen Silver, "'Two Different Sorts of Commerce'— Friendship and Strangership in Civil Society," in *Public and Private in Thought and Practice*, ed. Jeff Weintraub and Krishan Kumar (Chicago: University of Chicago Press, 1997), pp. 43–74.

4. Emotions Recollected

1. Daniel Kahneman, Ed Diener, and Norbert Schwarz, eds., *Well-Being: The Foundations of Hedonic Psychology* (New York: Russell Sage Foundation, 1999).
2. Avishai Margalit, *The Decent Society* (Cambridge: Harvard University Press, 1996).
3. Jon Elster, *Sour Grapes* (Cambridge: Cambridge University Press, 1983), chap. 2.
4. Jean Amery, *At the Mind's Limits*, trans. Sidney

Rosenfeld and Stella P. Rosenfeld (Bloomington: Indiana University Press, 1980), p. 22.

5. Ibid., p. 27.

6. William Wordsworth, "Preface to the Lyrical Ballads," in *English Romantic Poetry and Prose*, Appendix to the Preface, ed. Russell Noyes (New York: Oxford University Press, 1956), pp. 357–372.

7. Ibid., p. 361.

8. James Fenton, "Auden's Enchantment," in *New York Review of Books* 23, no. 3 (2000).

9. Charles Baudelaire, "L'Héautontimouroumenos," in *Selected Poems* (Middlesex: Penguin Books, 1975), trans. Joanna Richardson.

10. Sigmund Freud, *The Complete Psychological Works of Sigmund Freud*, trans. James Strachey (London: Hogarth Press, 1974), vol. 3, pp. 30–31, 148–149, 204–206; vol. 7, pp. 26–28.

11. David Hume, *A Dialogue Concerning Natural Religion*, ed. N. Kemp Smith (Indianapolis: Bobbs-Merrill, 1947), pp. 197–198. David Heyd, "Is Life Worth Reliving," in *Mind* 92 (1983): 21–37.

12. Daniel Kahneman, "Objective Happiness," in Kahneman et al., *Well-Being*, pp. 3–26.

13. Peter Goldie, *The Emotions* (Oxford: Oxford University Press, 2000).

14. Jean Paul Sartre, *Sketch for a Theory of the Emotions*, trans. Philip Mairet (London: Methuen, 1962).

5. A Moral Witness

1. Anna Akhmatova, "Instead of a Preface," trans. Stanley Kunitz and Max Hayward, in *Against Forgetting*, ed. Carolyn Forche (New York: W. W. Norton and Company, 1993), pp. 101–102.

2. Curzio Malparte, *Kaputt*, trans. Cesare Foligno (New York: E. P. Dutton, 1946).

3. G. E. M. Anscombe, "Modern moral philosophy," in *Philosophy* (1958): 1–18.

4. Carl Schmitt, *Political Theology: Four Chapters on the Concept of Sovereignty*, trans. George Schwab (Cambridge: MIT Press, 1985).

5. Mikhail Bakunin, *God and the State*, trans. Carlo Cafiero and Elisee Reclus (Columbus Junction, IA: E. H. Fulton, 1896).

6. Nadezhda Mandelstam, *Hope against Hope*, trans. Max Hayward (London: Collins-Harvill, 1971). Nadezhda Mandelstam, *Hope Abandoned*, trans. Max Hayward (New York: Athenaeum, 1974).

7. Victor Klemperer, *I Will Bear Witness: A Diary of the Nazi Years*, trans. Martin Chalmers, vol. 1: 1933–1941; vol. 2: 1942–1945 (New York: Random House, 1998).

8. Adam Czerniakow, *The Warsaw Diary of Adam Czernialow: Prelude to Doom*, ed. Raul Hilberg, Stanislaw Staron, and Josef Kermisz (New York: Stein and Day, 1979).

9. Klemperer, *I Will Bear Witness.*
10. Josephus Flavius, *The Jewish War,* trans. G. A. Williams (London: Penguin Classics, 1959), bk. 3, p. 361 (vii, 5).
11. Aleksandr Pushkin, *Boris Godunov,* introduction by Peter Ustinov (New York: Viking Press, 1982).
12. *Encyclopedia Judaica* (Jerusalem: Macmillan, 1971), vol. 3, p. 857.
13. Primo Levi, *The Drowned and the Saved,* trans. Raymond Rosenthal (New York: Summit Books, 1988).
14. Ludwig Wittgenstein, *Remarks on Frazer's Golden Bough* (Retford, Nottinghamshire, UK: Brynmill Press, 1983), p. 16.
15. Franz Werfel, *The Forty Days of Musa Dagh,* trans. Geoffrey Dunlop (New York: Modern Library, 1937).
16. Elena Lappin, "The man with two heads," *Granta* 66 (Summer 1999): 9–65.
17. Ibid., p. 46.
18. C. A. J. Coady, *Testimony: Philosophical Study* (Oxford: Clarendon Press, 1992).

6. Forgiving and Forgetting

1. I owe the distinction to Sidney Morgenbesser.
2. William Shakespeare, *Macbeth,* in *Oxford Standard Author's Shakespeare,* Act 2, scene ii, line 64.
3. Ludwig Wittgenstein, *Remarks on Frazer's Golden Bough* (Retford, Nottinghamshire, UK: Brynmill Press, 1983), p. 4e.

4. Moses Maimonides, *Mishneh Torah: The Book of Knowledge*, ed. Moses Hyamson (Jerusalem/New York: Feldheim Publishers, 1965), chap. 22, sec. 14, p. 83b.

5. Joseph Raz, *Practical Reason and Norms*, 2nd ed. (Oxford: Oxford University Press, 1999).

INDEX